# DAVID FAUST

# honest
# questions
# honest
# answers

## HOW TO ENGAGE IN COMPELLING CONVERSATIONS

### ABOUT YOUR CHRISTIAN FAITH

**Standard**®
PUBLISHING

Cincinnati, Ohio

Published by Standard Publishing, Cincinnati, Ohio
www.standardpub.com

Printed in: United States of America
Acquisitions editor: Dale Reeves
Cover design: Charles Brock, Faceout Studio
Interior design: Andrew Quach
Cover image © Shutterstock

ISBN 978-0-7847-3530-5

Library of Congress Cataloging-in-Publication Data

Faust, David.
Honest questions, honest answers : how to engage in compelling
conversations about your Christian faith / David Faust.
    p. cm.
  ISBN 978-0-7847-3530-5
1. Apologetics–Textbooks. 2. Christianity–Textbooks. 3. Witness bearing
(Christianity)–Textbooks. 4. Evangelistic work–Textbooks. I. Title.
  BT1107.F38 2012
  239–dc23
                        2012005463

17  16  15  14  13  12          1  2  3  4  5  6  7  8  9

*Honest Questions, Honest Answers* is, without question, one of the best—if not *the* best—apologetics books I've ever read. . . . It's very rare to find someone who can successfully combine the mind of an intellectual with the heart of an evangelist, but David Faust has done that well, creating a simple yet invaluable resource that's perfect for the atheist, agnostic, skeptic, or dedicated believer.

—Barry Cameron, senior pastor,
Crossroads Christian Church, Grand Prairie, Texas

I like this very readable book a lot. The questions are relevant, the answers are biblical, the applications are practical. David Faust rightly resists the postmodern temptation to doubt the reality of truth and the validity of reason. He writes not only from a solid academic background (an MA in apologetics) but also from many years of practical experience in dealing with doubters and seekers. What he has written here is of great benefit to us all.

—Jack Cottrell, professor of theology,
Cincinnati Christian University

Biblically backed up and lovingly written, this book is Dr. Faust at his customary best: accessible, helpful, cheerful, creative, personal, resolute, relatable . . . and honest. *Honest Questions, Honest Answers* presents apologetics without apologies, argues for Christ without being argumentative, and gives compelling reasons for faith in a world compelled to strangle faith with reason. This book is loaded!

—Bob Walters, author and Indianapolis newspaper columnist

David Faust writes from a wealth of experience—he has been in the trenches with folks of all ages who don't know Christ. His personality and loving, conversational demeanor are reflected throughout the pages of *Honest Questions, Honest Answers.* His deep concern for the lost—with practical application to reach them—is so evident. This book is a relevant blend of apologetics and evangelism.

—Dave Stone, senior pastor,
Southeast Christian Church, Louisville, Kentucky

*Honest Questions, Honest Answers* gives practical, tenable, life-defining answers to some of our most penetrating questions. This is a must-read for those who are searching for truth and for those who wish to accurately and lovingly defend it.

—Jeff Vines, senior pastor,
Christ's Church of the Valley, San Dimas, California

In characteristic fashion, David Faust brilliantly unravels some of today's most complex questions of faith. Best of all, the questions Dr. Faust tackles are *real* questions posed by *real* people. *Honest Questions, Honest Answers* is both refreshing and much needed in our contemporary culture. Whether you are genuinely seeking answers for yourself or want to help someone else, this book will help!

—Greg Marksberry, senior pastor,
First Church of Christ, Burlington, Kentucky

# Dedication

This book is dedicated to all who consider themselves doubters, seekers, inquirers, skeptics, and unbelievers; and to believers who ask honest questions about the Christian faith. May you discover for yourself that God "rewards those who earnestly seek him" (Hebrews 11:6).

# Acknowledgments

I am grateful to the individuals whose questions form the basis for this book. They are real people who graciously allowed me to interview them and include enough details to give the reader helpful glimpses into their personal lives and spiritual struggles. In some cases, names and details have been changed to protect their privacy.

All these individuals have moved further along in their spiritual journeys since asking the questions contained in the first edition of this book. Today some of them are committed Christians, while others remain unconvinced or have become firmer in their disbelief. Some of their questions are retrospective, reflecting the honest struggles these individuals experienced at the time of this book's original writing.

Thanks to Lynn Pratt, Dale Reeves, and others at Standard Publishing who have encouraged me by their careful editing, insightful suggestions, and prayerful vision for this book.

Finally, I am thankful for all of you who will use this book in your efforts to help others who are searching for hope. May the Lord give you courage, clarity, and confidence as you share your faith.

# Contents

# Getting Started:
## How to Use This Book

This was a hard book to write.

It wasn't hard to write because of its format. I enjoyed talking with the people whose questions appear in this book. Ordinary people have fascinating stories to tell, and we make a serious mistake if we don't listen carefully before telling others our own point of view. "Faith comes from hearing" (Romans 10:17), but many won't listen to us until first we've listened respectfully to them. The Bible says, "Be merciful to those who doubt" (Jude 22). We ought to feel grateful when our soul-searching friends are willing to open up and candidly share their honest questions.

This book wasn't hard to write because of the difficult issues it forced me to address—although I have to admit, the inquirers asked hard-hitting questions. When real people speak bluntly about their spiritual curiosity, their queries don't fit neatly into our preconceived theological categories. But tough questions do us a favor. They make us dig deeper to understand what we believe and why we believe it.

The thing that made this book hard to write wasn't the weight of the material; it was the weight of the responsibility. I feel a strong sense of responsibility to my friends and neighbors who don't know Christ. We who follow Christ need to do a better job of acquainting them with the God who loves them.

I also feel a strong responsibility toward Christians. There's never been a time when it was more urgent for believers to "give the reason for the hope that you have ... with gentleness and respect" (1 Peter 3:15). Jesus calls us to engage the world in spiritual battle, not retreat from it in fear. We must boldly take our faith into the tough arena of public conversation. There, the hard questions of real people will require from us every ounce of mental energy and love we can muster. And there, with God's help, we can build relationships and engage in compelling conversations that will lead our friends to the foot of the cross.

- This is an *apologetics book*. It explains some of the reasonable evidence that supports Christian faith.
- This is an *evangelism book*. It offers practical suggestions for engaging in compelling conversations with our friends.
- This is a *storybook*. It introduces us to real people and their honest questions.

By reading this book (or better yet, by sharing it with your spiritually searching friends) you can open the door for compelling conversations about your Christian faith.

## Take It Personally

Jesus instructed his followers to make disciples, baptize them, and teach them (Matthew 28:18-20), but how can we communicate our faith effectively in today's world? What approach should we use?

### It must be a personal approach

First Peter 3:15 is every Christian's responsibility: "In your hearts set apart Christ as Lord. Always be prepared to give an answer to everyone who asks you to give the reason for the hope that you have. But do this with gentleness and respect." All Christians can initiate conversations about spiritual issues, respond to questions posed by our non-Christian friends, and explain why we have hope. We need to be better equipped so that when someone asks about our faith, we can do more than merely refer the questioner to the church's pastoral staff. To communicate the gospel, we need to "take it personally" through one-on-one interaction with friends whose trust we have earned.

## It must be a loving approach

People resist evangelistic approaches that seem canned, preachy, or manipulative. This book advocates an apologetic of love. We need to defend our faith confidently and knowledgeably, but no persuasive argument will be successful without love. The apostle Paul said, "Knowledge puffs up, but love builds up" (1 Corinthians 8:1). And Jesus said, "By this all men will know that you are my disciples, if you love one another" (John 13:35). To lead others to Christ, we first need to hear their stories and concerns so we can understand where they're coming from. That's why each of this book's eight chapters also includes questions you can use for small group discussion or one-on-one conversation with a friend.

## It must be a respectful approach

When we encourage a friend to talk about his or her honest questions instead of squelching them, we fan the flame of spiritual curiosity and open doors for constructive dialogue. No one wins when our attempts at evangelism degenerate into angry tirades and personal attacks. "The Lord's servant must not quarrel; instead, he must be kind to everyone, able to teach, not resentful" (2 Timothy 2:24). Our goal isn't to win arguments, but to win souls.

## It must be a flexible approach

Instead of requiring you to memorize a one-size-fits-all evangelistic formula, this book provides a variety of questions and biblical facts you can use as talking points, depending on your friend's interests. The appendices in the back of the book address some additional misconceptions and questions you may encounter as you talk with others about the Christian faith.

### It must be a patient approach

Legendary performer Eddie Cantor said, "It takes twenty years to become an overnight success."[1] Spiritual growth sometimes happens rapidly, but it can't be forced by rushing someone into a decision he isn't ready to make. In America today most people come to Christ as a result of an ongoing process of relationship building and honest discussion rather than through a one-time encounter.

### It must be a biblical approach

Whatever outreach method we employ must keep the good news of Jesus Christ foremost. Scripture itself (particularly the book of Acts) sheds valuable light on the way we should interact with non-Christians.

### Let's Be Honest . . .

Since honesty is one of the themes of this book, I need to be honest about the limitations of what I have written. This volume focuses on some key issues non-Christians are asking about today, but it doesn't address every possible question. No doubt you could think of other important topics to add. This book is a pre-evangelism tool—a way to get started—a springboard for further discussion. Many Christians don't know how to initiate conversations about God and the Bible, so they never make an attempt. I hope this book helps you move beyond square one.

Frankly, I'm also concerned that someone might read the questions posed here, conclude that my answers are unsatisfactory, and find his own faith shaken. While I don't want to reinforce anyone's doubts, there's a greater danger if we don't talk openly about questions like the ones included here. Our non-Christian friends and neighbors ponder them more than we realize, and so do many Christians (more than we admit). Talking about doubt is the first step toward overcoming it. The Christian faith will stand up under close, critical examination. If you're not satisfied with my answers, that's all right—as long as you keep digging into God's Word to find better ones of your own.

The Master Teacher himself answers our questions better than anyone else, so before undertaking any kind of outreach effort, I urge you to pray and ask for the Lord's wisdom and guidance. Let the apostle Paul's words guide you: "Be wise in the way you act toward outsiders; make the most of every opportunity. Let your conversation be always full of grace, seasoned with salt, so that you may know how to answer everyone" (Colossians 4:5, 6).

Then as you make use of the main chapters in this book, be sure to take advantage of the additional information provided as well:

- **Appendices.** As you work through each chapter, check the appendices. These sections provide some additional material and a deeper look at many of the topics covered in the chapters.
- **Honest Questions for Personal Reflection / Group Discussion.** Questions at the end of every chapter are designed to help you or your small group relate to and reflect on the chapters—and then respond.
- **Resources for Further Study.** These recommended resources provided at the end of each chapter will help you see what other writers say about related topics.

No humanly devised methods will persuade our friends to accept Christ, but the basic tools of evangelism remain powerful and unchanged: truth and love; the sword of the Spirit (the Bible); the good news of a living Savior who lived, died, and rose for us. Our job is to plant and water gospel seeds in the hope that God will give the increase. If this book helps you do that, then the effort has been worthwhile.

# Questions People Ask

**Before I refuse to take your questions, I have an opening statement.**
**Ronald Reagan**

For as long as I can remember, I have asked a lot of questions. Growing up on a southern Ohio farm, I liked it when my parents took my two brothers and me on trips in our car. As we drove along, I'd fire question after question at my dad from my perch in the backseat:

- "Where are we going, Dad?"
- "How much longer, Dad?"
- "Can we stop at Dairy Queen, Dad?"

(I'm sure Dad appreciated those greatly.) I was fond of the why questions too.

- "Why is the sky blue?"
- "Why do we have to go to bed so early?"
- "Why do my older brothers get to do things I don't get to do?"

It's interesting how things work out. As the years went by, I got married, my wife and I had three children of our own, and we found ourselves on the receiving end of endless questions.

## Serious Questions

My youngest daughter, Melinda, was especially curious. She asked questions like, "What do lightning bugs do during the day?" and "Why don't birds get electrocuted when they sit on power lines?" (Now *that's* a great question!) One night as I tucked her into bed, she looked up at me thoughtfully and asked, "Dad, how do we know that Jesus is real?" I was glad to see her spiritual curiosity, but inwardly I breathed an anxious sigh, for I recalled the painful questions I had wrestled with in my own heart when I was a young man.

Even though I grew up in a Christian home, the teen years filled my mind with heavy questions:

- "How do I know there is a God?"
- "Does it really make sense to be a Christian?"
- "What about evolution?"
- "How do I know the Bible is true?"
- "Is my faith really my own, or is it merely a reflection of my parents' faith?"

At age seventeen my mind was absorbed with girls, basketball, music, and cars—but I also wondered about deeper issues. Sometimes at church it felt like Christians were playing games instead of interacting with the Lord of the universe, and I was frustrated with the shallowness and hypocrisy I sensed in myself and in others. Did we really mean the words we prayed? Were we serious about serving God 24/7 or just for a couple of hours on Sunday? I hungered to know: Is Christianity a worthy choice, or is it simply a waste of time? As a teen, I'd never heard of H. G. Wells. But I would have been intrigued by his comment: "If there is no God, nothing matters. If there is a God, nothing else matters!"[1] Instinctively I understood that if a God who created the universe really existed, he deserved more from me than just showing up on Sunday morning. If God really loved me—if he heard and answered prayer—then I wanted to know him and converse with him.

If God really guided the production of an inspired Book filled with divine wisdom and truth, I wanted to understand it. If life after death was more than a fantasy, I wanted to claim it as my own and help others discover it too.

But I also dared to look at the other side of the coin. Frankly, I reasoned, if God were nothing but a hoax and a lie, I didn't want to waste my life in religious game-playing.

During the summer before my senior year in high school, I began working for a tall, tan, muscular fellow named Ray. Now, Ray wasn't a theologian or a philosopher. He was a bricklayer, and a good one. He built houses and walls, fireplaces and chimneys. Ray gave me a job mixing mortar and carrying cement blocks for $2.50 an hour—not bad money for a seventeen-year-old in 1971. As we drove from job to job in Ray's red Chevy pickup truck, I asked him a lot of questions about life and faith. He didn't have all the answers, but he listened; and I listened to him as well. Ray's calm assurance about his faith earned my respect, and I noticed that the rugged men who worked for him tried to clean up their language when they were around him. I found Ray's commitment to Christ oddly reassuring, even though I continued to struggle with my own private doubts.

> The whole interest of reason, speculative as well as practical, is centred in the three following questions: 1. What can I know? 2. What ought I to do? 3. What may I hope?[2]
>
> Immanuel Kant

Sometimes that's all it takes—one real Christian who really believes, one person living a consistent life of faith—to make a difference in a seeker's heart.

At age eighteen I decided to attend a Christian college, not because I wanted to become a minister but because I wanted to find answers to satisfy my growing curiosity about my faith. During those college years I experienced the wonderful reality that God "rewards those who earnestly seek him" (Hebrews 11:6). Sometimes the rewards came in the form of wise words from godly instructors who patiently guided me through my valleys of uncertainty. They made me feel as if I were riding in the backseat of my dad's car again as I asked question after question and soaked up anything that might help me understand or explain my faith.

And along the way an interesting thing happened. The more answers I discovered, the more I found myself wanting to help other people with their spiritual journeys.

So I became a minister—and ended up in New York, of all places! I was a farm boy from Ohio, suddenly thrown into the challenging fray of a diverse urban culture. In my daily work I encountered skeptics, agnostics, free thinkers, and New Agers. I met Jehovah's Witnesses, Mormons, and followers of Sun Myung Moon's Unification Church. I got acquainted with Jewish rabbis who seemed shocked when they learned that I honestly believe Jesus is the Messiah promised in the Hebrew Scriptures.

After ten years in New York, I moved to Cincinnati to teach in a Christian college. During that time I also led in planting University Christian Church, an urban congregation serving students at the University of Cincinnati. There I dialogued with Hindus and Muslims; I preached to eager-minded young scholars studying engineering, mathematics, music, and art; and I led a small group attended by graduate students from the university medical school. As I listened to their comments, I discovered my new friends were asking the same kinds of questions I'd asked as a teenager: "Is God for real?" . . . "Is the Bible true?" . . .

## Questions Jesus Faced

Along the way, as I continued to study my Bible, I noticed how often people asked Jesus tough questions.

Jesus' first recorded words in the New Testament were a response to the question of his mother, Mary. His family had gone up to Jerusalem to celebrate the Passover Feast when he was twelve years old, and his parents inadvertently left him behind while they traveled a day's journey back toward their home in Nazareth. After searching for three days, they finally found him in the temple courts, sitting among the teachers, who were amazed at his understanding and his answers. With a motherly combination of relief and rebuke, Mary asked, "Son, why have you treated us like this? Your father and I have been anxiously searching for you."

And Jesus answered her question with two questions of his own: "Why were you searching for me? . . . Didn't you know I had to be in my Father's house?" (Luke 2:48, 49).

Mary and Joseph didn't understand what he meant, but young Jesus hadn't responded to them with insolence or rebellion. Despite his brilliance—he was the rare twelve-year-old who really *did* know more than his parents!—Jesus returned to Nazareth and continued to honor and obey Mary and Joseph (vv. 50-52).

During Jesus' public ministry, people constantly asked him questions. Some questions were sincere, asked by people who at least appeared to have a genuine interest in the truth.

- "What must I do to inherit eternal life?" asked the rich young ruler (Mark 10:17)—a good question, even though the young man later walked away from the Lord.
- "How can a man be born when he is old?" wondered Nicodemus (John 3:4)—and Jesus' intriguing answer proved convincing enough that Nicodemus later defended Jesus and apparently became a disciple (7:50-52; 19:38-42).
- "Who sinned, this man or his parents, that he was born blind?" (John 9:2), Jesus' disciples asked when they came upon a man who had been unable to see since birth. We might not have phrased the question quite the same way, but it's a legitimate issue nonetheless. Who hasn't wondered about the problem of evil and the cause of suffering?

Others came to Jesus with insincere questions cleverly designed to trap him in his words and make him look foolish. His debates with shrewd, hostile opponents make one of today's presidential press conferences look mild by comparison.

- "Why does your teacher eat with tax collectors and 'sinners'?" (Matthew 9:11). The Pharisees asked Jesus' disciples that question, trying to stir up doubt and controversy.
- "Is it right to pay taxes to Caesar or not?" (Matthew 22:17). Others touched the sensitive nerves of nationalistic pride and hatred of taxation when they asked Jesus that.
- "Teacher, which is the greatest commandment in the Law?" Even that important question came from a lawyer whose main intent was to test Jesus (Matthew 22:34-36).

The Lord answered each inquiry with amazing wisdom and disarming honesty.

## Questions Jesus Asked, Answers He Didn't Give

Jesus was good at asking questions too.

- He began a life-changing conversation with the Samaritan woman at the well with a simple request: "Will you give me a drink?" (John 4:7). And before their encounter was over, she began to comprehend what he meant when he offered her "living water."
- In his Sermon on the Mount, Jesus humorously illustrated the futility of judging others, by asking, "Why do you look at the speck of sawdust in your brother's eye and pay no attention to the plank in your own eye?" (Matthew 7:3).
- In response to the query "Who is my neighbor?" Jesus told his well-known story about the Good Samaritan, and then drove home the point with a question of his own: "Which of

these three [the priest, Levite, or Samaritan] do you think was a neighbor to the man who fell into the hands of robbers?" (Luke 10:29, 36).

So adept was Jesus at responding to public scrutiny and debate that the day finally came when "no one dared to ask him any more questions" (Matthew 22:46).

Jesus even knew when *not* to answer a question! He amazed Governor Pilate when he refused to answer the accusations false witnesses flung at him (Mark 15:5; John 19:9). Likewise, during Jesus' trial, King Herod, hoping to see him perform some miracle, "plied him with many questions, but Jesus gave him no answer" (Luke 23:8, 9). Pardon the mixed metaphor, but for Jesus to engage in serious dialogue with "that fox" Herod would have been like throwing "pearls to pigs" (see Luke 13:31-33; Matthew 7:6).

On one occasion, the Jewish chief priests and elders demanded, "By what authority are you doing these things? . . . And who gave you this authority?"

Jesus wisely replied, "I will also ask you one question. If you answer me, I will tell you by what authority I am doing these things. John's baptism—where did it come from? Was it from heaven, or from men?"

Good question. But instead of answering it immediately, Jesus' adversaries slinked away and held a committee meeting. They discussed it among themselves and said, "If we say, 'From heaven,' he will ask, 'Then why didn't you believe him?' But if we say, 'From men'—we are afraid of the people, for they all hold that John was a prophet." So they dismissed their meeting, marched back to Jesus, and announced their conclusion: "We don't know."

And Jesus said, "Neither will I tell you by what authority I am doing these things" (Matthew 21:23-27).

End of discussion!

Jesus wisely understood the balance expressed in two proverbs. The first says, "Do not answer a fool according to his folly, or you will be like him yourself." In other words, there are times when it's best not to answer a question asked with impure motives. But the proverb in the very next verse indicates that sometimes we must speak up: "Answer a fool according to his folly, or he will be wise in his own eyes" (Proverbs 26:4, 5).

Jesus was always ready to wrestle with tough issues in the give-and-take of public dialogue. He didn't shrink back from debate, but always handled himself with wisdom and grace. So should we.

## Questions We Will Face

Since we are called to follow in the footsteps of Jesus, we need to look carefully at the kinds of questions he faced, for they serve as prototypes for the kinds of questions we may encounter as well.

I've discovered that people usually ask questions that fall into one of the following five major categories.

### Philosophical questions

"Wait a minute," you may say. "I'm not a philosopher. I probably know more about Play-Doh than Plato! I don't sit around pondering the meaning of life." Don't sell yourself short. You don't have to be a card-carrying member of the American Philosophical Association to wonder about questions like these:

- "Where is the God of justice?" (Malachi 2:17).
- "If a man dies, will he live again?" (Job 14:14).
- "What is truth?" (John 18:38).

Admittedly, some Christians don't like to talk about philosophy. The word rarely appears in the Bible, and when it does, it's used in a negative sense to describe hollow and deceptive human ideas that oppose the revealed Word of God (see 1 Corinthians 1:20; Colossians 2:8). But at its root, the word *philosophy* simply means "love of wisdom" (from the Greek *philos* plus *sophia*).[3] And since God wants us all to be lovers of wisdom (as the book of Proverbs makes clear), we need to pay attention to the philosophical trends of our culture so we'll make wise decisions and "take captive every thought to make it obedient to Christ" (2 Corinthians 10:5).

## Theological questions

You don't consider yourself a theologian? Neither did Anthony. When I met him, he was employed as a detective for the New York City Transit Police. A tall, tough-looking individual with a thick Italian accent and a gun strapped to his ankle, Anthony engaged in daily work that included investigating subway suicides and muggings. When he and his wife started coming to my home for Bible studies, their questions were hard-hitting and heartfelt: "Why is there so much evil in the world?" . . . "How can anybody be hopeful anymore, when people can be so cruel?" . . . "Does God really care?" Accustomed to seeing life at its worst, Anthony couldn't be satisfied with a naive, unquestioning faith.

Jesus dealt deftly with tricky theological questions like, "Lord, are only a few people going to be saved?" (Luke 13:23, 24). And in his ministry with new Christians, the apostle Paul found it necessary to respond to numerous inquiries about doctrinal issues like the Lord's Supper, spiritual gifts, and the resurrection (see 1 Corinthians 11–15). To handle questions like these, we need to be diligent students of the Scripture who correctly handle the word of truth (2 Timothy 2:15).

## Ethical questions

First-century Christians wondered, "Is it better to marry or remain single?" and "Is it OK to eat meat that previously was offered as a sacrifice to idols?" (see 1 Corinthians 7, 8). Christians today continue to face questions about tough ethical issues. How should Christians respond to the global financial crisis? Where should we stand on abortion and homosexuality? Is assisted suicide permissible? What does the Bible say about environmental issues, racism, and economic justice?

## Hypothetical questions

There always have been people who ask questions simply for argument's sake, not because they really want to know the answer. Have you ever encountered someone like that? Perhaps it's a coworker filled with casual curiosity, who quizzes you about your faith but always manages to shrug off your invitations to attend a Bible study or church service. Maybe it's a classmate who loves to get the professor to go off on a tangent by diverting the class lecture down some pointless side alley. Or maybe you have a skeptical friend who delights in asking theoretical brainteasers like, "If God can do anything, can he make a rock so big he can't lift it?"

Some folks simply enjoy a stimulating argument. They would agree with the eighteenth-century philosopher Joseph Joubert, who said, "It is better to debate a question without settling it than to settle a question without debating it."[4]

Jesus faced a classic hypothetical question when some men described the following situation: "'Teacher,' they said, 'Moses told us that if a man dies without having children, his brother must marry the widow and have children for him. Now there were seven brothers among us. The first one married and died, and since he had no children, he left his wife to his brother. The same thing happened to the second and third brother, right on down to the seventh. Finally, the woman died. Now then, at the resurrection, whose wife will she be of the seven, since all of them were married to her?'" (Matthew 22:24-28).

A complicated scenario indeed! But wait a minute—who were the people who came to Jesus with this clever question? They were "the Sadducees, who say there is no resurrection" (v. 23). Here they were, asking a complicated riddle about life after death, when they had already presupposed that no resurrection was possible in the first place!

Cutting to the heart of the real issue, Jesus replied, "You are in error because you do not know the Scriptures or the power of God." However, Jesus didn't evade their question. At the resurrection, he explained, "people will neither marry nor be given in marriage; they will be like the angels in heaven" (and angels, evidently, are quite content to be single).

Then the Lord quickly returned to the bigger issue: "But about the resurrection of the dead—have you not read what God said to you, 'I am the God of Abraham, the God of Isaac, and the God of Jacob'?" In other words, when God spoke to Moses at the burning bush hundreds of years after Abraham, Isaac, and Jacob died, he still could identify himself as their God—for these men were still living in God's presence even after death.

Jesus then put to rest this hypothetical question when he pointed out that God "is not the God of the dead but of the living." And the crowds "were astonished at his teaching" (vv. 29-33).

## Personal questions

At some point, we all wonder about the significance of our own lives. The book of Ecclesiastes begins with this brutally honest refrain: "'Meaningless! Meaningless!' says the Teacher. 'Utterly meaningless! Everything is meaningless'" (Ecclesiastes 1:2). Let's face it. Life does seem meaningless at times—especially if there's no divine reference point to help it all make sense. Many of our friends and neighbors face each new morning with the kind of inner *dis-ease* (a lack of ease) Moses warned that the people of ancient Israel would experience if they denied God: "The LORD will give you an anxious mind, eyes weary with longing, and a despairing heart. You will live in constant suspense, filled with dread both night and day, never sure of your life. In the morning you will say, 'If only it were evening!' and in the evening, 'If only it were morning!'" (Deuteronomy 28:65-67).

Anxiety and discontent are nothing new. But dis-eases like these have reached a new level of intensity today. In a post-9/11 world, terrorism remains a constant threat; routine travel means extra inconvenience and stress; and the global economy is a mess with no long-term solutions in sight. In extreme cases, personal despair boils over like a volcano. More often, it just lingers like a cold fog, stealing hope from the hearts of young and old who sense that life should consist of more than the routines of work to do and bills to pay, punctuated by the short-lived, counterfeit joy of occasional parties and holidays. There must be more to life than that, they think. And they're right.

## Honest Answers

While serving as a minister in New York, I received a phone call one day from a woman with an interesting request.

"You don't know me," she began, "but I've heard that you're willing to speak to different groups about Christian faith."

"Yes," I replied, privately wondering what I was about to get myself into.

"My husband and I have a little group of friends who share a common interest in finding out more about different faiths," she continued. "Would you be willing to come and talk to our group about what it means to be a Christian?"

"Sure," I said. And a few days later, my wife and I sat in our new friends' house, dining on authentic Greek food—lamb, feta cheese, stuffed grape leaves. After dinner we headed downstairs to their large basement where, to my amazement, their "little" group of friends continued to grow until about fifty people had crowded into the room and sat on folding chairs. As they greeted me, some of the guests identified themselves as atheists, some as disenchanted Catholics, some as Jewish. Others said they were Greek Orthodox, and some simply called themselves seekers.

After quieting everyone down, our hosts announced, "Everybody, this is Dave Faust. He's come here tonight with his wife, Candy, to talk to us about his faith as a Christian." Then turning to me warmly, they said, "Dave, tell us what you believe."

Now, I hadn't prepared a fancy speech. Thinking quickly, I came up with a simple outline that focused on three key points: why I love Jesus, why I love the Bible, and why I love the church. Not particularly controversial topics—or so I thought. But after I spoke for about half an hour, the group kept me standing on the floor for another ninety minutes of vigorous questions and answers. Like Paul at Athens, I was "bringing some strange ideas to [their] ears, and [they wanted] to know what they [meant]" (Acts 17:20). By the time my wife and I said our good-byes and left that night (with an invitation to return again at a future date), I was more convinced than ever that spiritual curiosity is alive and well in our culture.

I've never forgotten those curious questioners gathered in that basement. I think Simon Peter had people like them in mind when he urged, "Always be prepared to give an answer to everyone who asks you to give the reason for the hope that you have" (1 Peter 3:15). The *reason* for our hope—that's what our friends and neighbors seek from us. Not a prepared speech. Not impressive-sounding intellectual arguments. Not a canned evangelistic sales pitch. Not hollow, pious-sounding religious answers to questions no one's really asking.

They want to know why they should bother to get up in the morning and face another day. They want to know whether God is real—and if he is, what difference does he make in ordinary life? In their honest moments of introspection, they want to know if life after death is more than just a pipe dream.

To people like these, we Christians dare to make an audacious claim. We say there is indeed a God who is there and the reality of God makes all the difference. We say there's hope.

People in your family and your neighborhood want to know why.

We need to give them honest answers.

# Honest Questions for Personal Reflection

1. The thought of defending my faith makes me feel . . .

2. One situation in which I defended my faith was . . .

3. One question I'd like to ask God is . . .

# Honest Questions for Group Discussion

## Relate

1. What was your exposure to spiritual things when you were a child? Were your parents people of faith? What church or religious group influenced you? Did you learn about God and the Bible in Sunday school? What were your impressions, either good or bad?

2. How would you describe your attitude about spiritual things now? Check the one that most applies.

_____ Mild curiosity—I think spiritual issues are important, but I'm not looking to be converted to anything.

_____ Strong interest—I think spiritual issues are important, and I'm eager to grow in my personal faith.

_____ Disillusioned—I've been burned by my past religious involvement, so I tend to be pretty cautious about making any commitments.

_____ Doubtful—I'm not sure there's much spiritual truth to be known.

_____ Firm contentment—I feel very settled and convinced about my faith.

## Reflect

3. Read and react to the following Bible verses:

- Matthew 7:7, 8. Jesus encouraged his disciples to ask and seek and knock. When you think about your own spiritual growth, what are you seeking right now?

- Hebrews 11:6. How does God reward those who earnestly seek him?

4. Read Acts 17:2, 3, 17 and 18:4, 19. The apostle Paul often "reasoned" with others about the gospel. Have you ever done this? Explain.

5. What is the hardest question anyone ever asked you about God, the Bible, or the church? What did you say in response? Did your answer satisfy your questioner? Explain. If you had it to do over again, what would you do differently?

6. Peter and John said, "We cannot help speaking about what we have seen and heard" (Acts 4:20). How do you feel about defending or sharing your faith? Check the one that most applies.

\_\_\_\_ excited and eager
\_\_\_\_ fearful and unprepared
\_\_\_\_ frustrated and anxious
\_\_\_\_ other:

## Respond

7. Read aloud 1 Peter 3:15. Which part of this verse do you need to apply in your life during the coming week? Why? How will you do it?

\_\_\_\_ set apart Christ as Lord in my heart

\_\_\_\_ prepare myself to give answers to others who ask about my faith

\_\_\_\_ set a better example in my daily life so others will want to ask me about my faith

\_\_\_\_ defend my faith with greater gentleness and respect

# Resources for Further Study

*Dinner with Skeptics: Defending God in a World That Makes No Sense* by Jeff Vines (Joplin, MO: College Press, 2008)

*How Do You Know You're Not Wrong?: Responding to Objections That Leave Christians Speechless* by Paul Copan (Grand Rapids, MI: Baker Books, 2005)

*Letters from a Skeptic: A Son Wrestles with His Father's Questions About Christianity* by Gregory Boyd and Edward Boyd (Colorado Springs, CO: David C. Cook, new edition 2008)

*Mere Christianity* by C. S. Lewis (New York: HarperCollins, 2001). Lewis's classic work in defense of Christianity.

*On Guard: Defending Your Faith with Reason and Precision* by William Lane Craig (Colorado Springs, CO: David C. Cook, new edition 2010)

*The Case for Faith: A Journalist Investigates the Toughest Objections to Christianity* by Lee Strobel (Grand Rapids, MI: Zondervan, 2000)

*The Faith Once For All: Bible Doctrine for Today* by Jack Cottrell (Joplin, MO: College Press, 2002). A systematic theology book that's both scholarly and easy to understand.

*The Reason for God: Belief in an Age of Skepticism* by Timothy Keller (New York: Riverhead Books, 2009)

*When Skeptics Ask: A Handbook on Christian Evidences* by Norman Geisler and Ronald Brooks (Grand Rapids, MI: Baker Books, reprint 2008)

## Chapter 2

# Is the Bible Really True?

I was thinking about how people seem to read the Bible a whole lot more as they get older. Then it dawned on me—they're cramming for their final exam.
**George Carlin**

In Australia to speak for a church-sponsored retreat, I had strolled into the retreat center's dining hall where lunch was being served. Still adjusting to jet lag but eager to experience Australian culture, I sat down next to a young man and struck up a conversation. I soon learned that my new friend, Ben, was twenty-three years old. While sipping pumpkin soup, we talked about cricket, rugby, and American football ("footy," or "gridiron," as the Aussies call it).

Ben asked me what I did in America. When I told him I was a Bible teacher, a skeptical look swept across his face. "The Bible!" he said. "You can't believe a thing that's in that book!"

Calmly I said, "Well, I disagree. I think you *can* trust the Bible. Would you like to talk about this some more?"

He would, and we did. I wondered why Ben was attending the retreat, in light of his skepticism. But I soon discovered he was willing—even eager—to talk about spiritual things. And later, when I decided to write a book filled with honest questions people ask about Christian faith, I knew I needed to include Ben's story.

## What's Beyond the Border?

"I'm willing to talk about these things," Ben said, "but Christians annoy me when they try to push their opinions on me. If I want to know something, I'll ask them."

"When I was about eight I went to Sunday school," he remembered. "But it started at nine o'clock, and I just wanted to stay in bed. The only reason I went was that my mother pushed me to go. Finally, I told her I just didn't want to go anymore."

I asked whether Ben believed in God. He said, "I don't believe in him, but I don't disbelieve in him either. I have no idea whether he's real or not. I have a lot of questions about the very beginning of life—you know, how did we get here in the first place?—and about whether there is such a thing as an afterlife. I don't really believe in life after death. I don't see how we're any different from animals. As far as I know, when you die you go six feet under the ground and have worms crawling out your eyes."

"Everything has to start somewhere," Ben continued, "no matter what it is. Basically the world is like a picture in a frame. It has to have a border where it finishes. And what's outside the border, nobody knows. Nobody's been able to go that far into space."

## Show Me the Facts

What was Ben's biggest question about Christian faith?

"People always say that God has told them this, that, or whatever, and I really can't see how. I guarantee that you can't actually hear him. You can't actually see him. You can't actually touch him. Some people say, 'I just know in my heart that he's told me to do this.' But the way I see it, that's just a gut feeling they have because they want to do something."

I asked Ben whether he believed the Bible is God's Word.

"I don't take anybody's word for anything, straight up!" Ben immediately responded, and the swift barrage of comments that followed made it clear that this topic hit a nerve. "If the Bible is true, prove it to me. I don't believe it. Anybody could have written it. I wouldn't trust it. There's no actual proof for it. 'Have faith'—that's what I've been told many times. But I don't believe in something I have no proof for. It doesn't matter what it is."

Ben conceded that some of what's recorded in the Bible might actually have happened. He said, "They might really have stoned someone or stabbed someone or whatever. But people living in those times could have just written it down and made a story out of it. The writers don't really give any proof of God. All other history books are based on facts—physical events that actually happened. But the whole God thing isn't like that. There's no reason to believe that God came down and spoke to Moses on the mountain. I don't see how that actually happened."

## Hard to Believe

Softening his tone a bit, Ben went on: "The Bible says a lot of good things that relate to life. But I don't think you can see it as reliable."

Ben explained his concern this way: "If you get ten different people to read the Bible, you might come out with ten different versions. Even though they're reading the same words, they interpret them in an entirely different way. That makes it harder to believe. I have to admit that the Christian interpretation seems a lot better than some of the other ones I've heard about. But if God actually wrote the Bible, he'd make it so everyone could understand it in the same way. If he wanted somebody to know something, he'd make it plain."

Ben found it hard to believe the prophecies of the Bible too. He said, "People keep pointing to the Bible and predicting there's going to be doomsday or World War III, but nothing's happened so far."

How much of the Bible had he read at the time? "Maybe half of it."

Ben works for a boat-building firm during the week. And despite his doubts, he still goes to church occasionally on the weekends. He has a lot of friends there, including the minister. He smiled as he said, "I'm sort of the resident atheist, I guess." He doesn't consider himself an enemy of Christians, but at least for now he can't accept their faith as his own.

"I think the Bible tells us some good points to live by," he has concluded, "but a lot of stuff in there is hard to believe. And some of it even seems impossible."

Ben hasn't found the answers he craves, but at least he's asking some worthwhile questions. How can we help him (or others like him) trust in the reliability of God's Word? Let's start with some information about the uniqueness of the Bible—some basic facts no one can deny.

## The Bible Deserves at Least a Fair Hearing

There are plenty of other religious books a person can read. But it's hard to find a book (of any kind) that has the credentials of the Bible.

Jesus said his words would never pass away (Mark 13:31), and the Bible has fulfilled that prophecy. It's proven to be indestructible. The Bible has survived many things:

- time (even though most of it was written on perishable materials like leather and papyrus)
- persecution (Roman emperors like Diocletian ordered copies of the Bible destroyed)
- criticism (What other book has endured so much scrutiny?)
- the negligence of its friends (Christians who seldom read it)
- the animosity of its enemies (Communist governments who have suppressed its publication and distribution)
- false systems that have been built on it (like cults that twist its meaning, or slave owners who tried to use the Bible to justify slavery)

Critics keep pounding on the Bible, but like an anvil, God's Word endures while the skeptics' hammers wear out.

Individual lives and entire cultures have been changed by the Bible's message. Bible-believing people founded many of the world's finest educational institutions. Visit poverty-stricken nations like Haiti and Ethiopia, and observe the vast amount of medical and vocational assistance being offered in Jesus' name by native-born Christians and missionaries from other lands. Visit a law library and ponder the fact that many of our nation's laws are grounded in moral principles as old as the Ten Commandments. Consider the impact of biblical themes on great music and art, from Handel's *Messiah* to Michelangelo's statue *David*. Look around at the hospitals, schools, and senior-care facilities in your town begun and supported by Bible-believing people, and notice how Bible believers so often show up to help with disaster relief and other forms of community service. And who can count all the individuals whose lives have been made whole because of their faith?

Even the English language has been influenced by Scripture, for many of our everyday expressions originated in the Bible:

- "the handwriting on the wall" (Daniel 5:5)
- "the apple of my eye" (Deuteronomy 32:10; Psalm 17:8)
- "an eye for an eye" (Exodus 21:24)
- "scapegoat" (Leviticus 16:6-10, 20-22)
- "a Good Samaritan" (Luke 10:25-37)
- "a thorn in the flesh" (2 Corinthians 12:7)[1]

The Bible has earned the admiration of literary scholars for its poetry (Psalm 23); for its probing evaluation of deep subjects like the problem of evil (Job); and for its impartiality and frankness about its heroes and their flaws (reporting honestly about Noah's drunkenness, Abraham's lies, David's adultery, and Peter's denials of Christ). And it has received tributes from great thinkers like Abraham Lincoln ("I believe the Bible is the best gift God has ever given to man") and Sir Isaac Newton ("There are more sure marks of authenticity in the Bible than in any profane history").[2]

While all this will not convince a skeptic that the Bible is God's Word, it demonstrates that it's unreasonable to ignore or belittle the Bible. If God were to reveal himself through a written book, we would expect that book to be unique, and that's exactly what we find in the Bible. Its basic message is simple enough for a child to understand, yet challenging enough that a scholar can never fully plumb its depths. This Book deserves a fair hearing.

## Just the Facts

Evolutionist Aldous Huxley said, "Facts do not cease to exist because they are ignored."[3] Unfortunately, many people have never considered the multitude of facts that support the truthfulness of the Bible.

Unlike legends or fairy tales that start with "once upon a time," the events recorded in the Bible occurred in real places, and many of them have been substantiated by other historical documents.

- Moses lived in Egypt and walked on Mount Sinai.
- Jesus was born in Bethlehem and grew up in the village of Nazareth.
- Jesus walked the streets of Jerusalem and healed a disabled man by the pool of Bethesda.
- Jesus sailed with his disciples on the Sea of Galilee and sat with a Samaritan woman beside Jacob's well in Samaria.
- The apostle Paul visited Rome, Ephesus, and Athens.

Since those places still exist, the accuracy of the Bible events in regard to travel times, relation of one locale to another, and even the end result of a predicted destruction (Nineveh, for example) can be verified today. The Bible's history lays itself open for critical examination.

Luke, a medical doctor who wrote the Gospel of Luke and the book of Acts, has earned wide respect for his historical and geographical accuracy. Luke's frequent mentions of well-known government officials and regional boundaries invite historical scrutiny, and strong evidence supports the beloved physician's precision time after time. According to biblical scholar Norman Geisler, "Luke names thirty-two countries, fifty-four cities, and nine islands without making a single error"[4] in geographical placement. He also gives correct titles for a wide variety of government officials, like "governor" and "tetrarch" (Luke 3:1), "politarch" or "city official" (Acts 17:6), "proconsul" (Acts 18:12-17), and "protos" or "chief official" of the island (Acts 28:7).

A few years ago I decided to put the Bible to my own little historical test. I read through the book of Acts and jotted down references to people and events that might have some corroboration outside the New Testament. Then I spent several hours in the dusty recesses of a library reference room, checking to see whether other ancient historians backed up Luke's testimony. What I discovered strongly reinforced my conviction that the Bible is telling the truth. Here are some samples:

- Candace, queen of the Ethiopians (Acts 8:27), was mentioned by the ancient writer Strabo, who said that Candace was "ruler of the Ethiopians in my time—a masculine sort of woman, and blind in one eye."[5]
- Herod Agrippa's gruesome death (Acts 12:19-23) was described in gory detail by Josephus, a Jewish historian who lived from about AD 37 to 100. The Bible says the king was struck down and eaten by worms because he accepted worship instead of giving praise to God. Josephus says the king didn't rebuke his flatterers when they called him a god, and "a severe pain also arose in his belly, and began in a most violent manner."[7]

> There is no ground at all for refusing to accept these oldest traditions [the Bible] as historically trustworthy in all essentials, and in their chronological ordering of history.[6]
>
> Edward Meyer

- Roman historical biographer Suetonius corroborated the fact that Emperor Claudius expelled the Jews from Rome, as reported in Acts 18:2.[8]
- Acts 24:24 mentions Governor Felix and his wife Drusilla. According to various historians, Drusilla was directly related to Antony and Cleopatra.[9]

In the Bible lands today, you can visit archaeological sites that illustrate how the story of the Bible intertwines with other historical events.

- Wade through King Hezekiah's tunnel, first mentioned in 2 Kings 20:20.
- View the more than two-thousand-year-old Isaiah scroll found among the Dead Sea Scrolls, which provides important evidence for the text of this ancient Book.
- Sit in the great theater in Ephesus mentioned in Acts 19:28, 29.
- Walk through the marketplace in Corinth, where members of the Corinthian church shopped.
- Stand on the Areopagus in Athens where Paul preached (Acts 17:22-31).

The Bible's historical accuracy offers impressive evidence that the Book deserves our trust. Other important lines of evidence support the truthfulness of the Bible as well.

## Prophet Sharing

In the book of Acts, Christians often pointed to fulfilled prophecies as evidence to support their preaching about Christ. These prophecies could not have been mere guesswork. For one thing, anyone who claimed to be a true messenger of God had to speak with complete accuracy or risk being executed by stoning (Deuteronomy 18:20-22). Needless to say, a man or woman aware of this law would think twice before presuming to speak on God's behalf!

Biblical prophecies dealt with information far beyond the range of scientific calculation or ordinary guessing, and they often included remarkably specific details. For example, the prophet Isaiah twice mentioned a Persian ruler named Cyrus (who ruled in the mid-500s BC),[10] even though strong evidence suggests that Isaiah wrote his book around 700 BC—more than a century before Cyrus was even born! (See

Isaiah 44:28–45:1 and Ezra 1:1-4, which includes Ezra's historical record of Cyrus's deeds.)

Consider the track record of these prophets:

- Elijah predicted a major drought. There was neither rain nor dew for three and a half years, until Elijah announced that it was going to rain (1 Kings 17, 18; James 5:17, 18).

- Nahum predicted numerous details about the downfall of the Assyrian capital city of Nineveh that came true in astonishing detail. These facts are easily verifiable today (Nahum 1–3).[11]

- Ezekiel predicted numerous details about the downfall of the city of Tyre long before it happened (Ezekiel 26).[12]

- Daniel not only could interpret dreams with amazing accuracy; he could tell what someone else dreamed in the first place! This amazing feat convinced even a pagan king that God was the source of Daniel's information (Daniel 2).

- Micah foretold the Messiah's birthplace with enough clarity that King Herod's advisers could point the Magi toward Bethlehem (Micah 5:2; Matthew 2:1-6).

- David provided an accurate description of Jesus' crucifixion centuries before it occurred, including the fact that lots were cast for Jesus' clothing (Psalm 22:18; compare John 19:23, 24) and Jesus' words spoken from the cross: "My God, my God, why have you forsaken me?" (Psalm 22:1; compare Matthew 27:46).

- Isaiah foretold the crucifixion with such vivid details that it almost reads like a page from the New Testament! Isaiah 53 mentions that Jesus was "pierced for our transgressions" (v. 5; compare John 19:34) and was "with the rich in death" (v. 9; compare Matthew 27:57-61).

My friend Ben complained that "people keep pointing to the Bible and predicting there's going to be doomsday or World War III, but nothing's happened so far." But when thoughtful Christians speak of biblical prophecy, we're not making lame speculations about what an erratic Middle Eastern leader might do. We're talking about facts that shine from the pages of history like permanent miracles to behold. Actually Ben's comment sounds similar to another prophecy made in Scripture "In the last days scoffers will come. . . . They will say, 'Where is this "coming" he promised? . . . Everything goes on as it has since the beginning of creation'" (2 Peter 3:3, 4).

By simply saying the word, God created the universe and later destroyed the earth with the great flood of Noah's day. And God has stated that the present heavens and earth are going to be destroyed by that same powerful word (2 Peter 3:5-7). We don't know when the end will occur, but based on the Lord's track record of accuracy, we're wise to be prepared. It's going to happen (Mark 13:32-37). In Matthew 24, Jesus' teachings about the end of the world are interwoven with predictions that already have been fulfilled in the destruction of Jerusalem, which took place in AD 70 under a Roman general named Titus.[13]

The Bible acknowledges that false prophets will arise (Jeremiah 23:16-32; Matthew 7:21-23; 24:4, 5, 24). This fact does not negate God's ability to know the past, the present, and the future, as he claims in his Word (Isaiah 46:9, 10). The Bible's prophecies underscore the reliability of the entire volume. As the apostle Peter put it, "Prophecy never had its origin in the will of man, but men spoke from God as they were carried along by the Holy Spirit" (2 Peter 1:21).

## Science Facts, Not Science Fiction

In 1994 an Australian Parks and Wildlife Service officer named David Noble stumbled onto a grove of thirty-nine trees in the Wollemi National Park rain forest preserve near Sydney.[14] The trees, nicknamed Wollemi Pines, were dubbed one of the most important botanical finds of the twentieth century because they represent a plant species that experts thought had become extinct centuries ago. One environmental expert commented, "The fact that such a large plant can go undiscovered for so long is a clear indication that there is more work to be done before we can say we understand our environment." Ironically, *Wollemi* is an aboriginal word that means "look around you."

Look around you? Yes, that's what Christians say to do: look at nature and look at the Bible, and you will discover that God's *works* do not contradict God's *words.* The same God who created the universe also inspired the Scriptures. What God has said in the Bible harmonizes with what he's done in creation.

Our word *science* comes from the Latin *scientia,* which means "knowledge." God was the first scientist. In fact, as theologians point out, God alone is capable of omniscience (*omni* means "all"). He's the "omni-scientist," the only one who possesses all knowledge of nature. "The fear of the LORD," the Bible points out, "is the beginning of knowledge" (Proverbs 1:7); the word "knowledge" there is *scientiae* in the Latin Vulgate.[15]

Christian faith isn't unscientific or antiscientific. For one thing, Christians acknowledge the contributions of science. We benefit as much as anyone else from LASIK eye surgery, state-of-the-art dental care, and coronary bypass procedures. We use smartphones and tablet computers, cook with microwaves, and appreciate air-conditioned homes and cars. God is the one who created physical laws for us to discover and use. To engage in good science is, as astronomer Johannes Kepler said, "to think God's thoughts after him."[16]

But unlike those who practically make a god out of science, we insist that science has its limitations. Because today's foregone conclusion often becomes tomorrow's discarded theory, the truly scientific mind must be humble about its conclusions, not arrogant. Some individuals seem to live by two basic rules:

1. Science holds the answers to all the questions of life.
2. Anyone who does not believe rule number one is not scientific.

But if science alone were the key to life, Solomon would have discovered it, since he possessed unsurpassed knowledge of botany, biology and other sciences (1 Kings 4:29-34). Yet all his scientific knowledge left him empty and still grasping for the meaning of life, observing that everything seemed "meaningless" (Ecclesiastes 1:2). Science and the Bible can be useful allies, for the very questions science alone cannot answer—questions about the worth and purpose of human life, our origin and destiny—are the very questions the Bible seeks to answer.

Does the Bible have anything to say about modern science? More than we often realize.

- The first book of the Bible indicates that the stars are uncountable (Genesis 15:5).
- Another early text, Job 26:7, speaks of the earth being suspended in space.
- Isaiah 40:22 mentions "the circle of the earth."
- Today we know how blood circulates water, oxygen, and nourishment to the cells of our bodies, but centuries ago God's Word stated, "The life of a creature is in the blood" (Leviticus 17:11; also see v. 14).

The idea that the eternal God has always been alive fits well with the scientific law of biogenesis, the principle that all life comes from previously existing life. And the order and complexity of nature fit better with the concept of a wise Creator than with the macroevolutionary hypothesis that credits creation to an impersonal force plus time plus chance.

The Bible provides a helpful frame of reference for science; for unlike other religious worldviews, the Scripture insists that the physical world is real (not an illusion), that it was created good (Genesis 1), but that it is not God or a part of God (and so it's a legitimate object of study and innovation, not an object of worship).

## Making It Easy

Since Christ himself is the theme of the Bible, here's an acrostic I've used to help me remember some of the points we've just gone through.

**C**laims. The Bible authors repeatedly say they're communicating God's Word. While this claim alone doesn't prove the Bible is true, we need to understand the authors' intent. If we hold that the Bible is nothing more than a human book, we contradict what the Bible itself claims to be.

**H**istorical accuracy. Archaeological evidence supports the accuracy of the Old and New Testaments.

**R**emarkable style. Many readers find that the Bible rings true because of its frankness and its spiritual power.

**I**ndestructibility. This 2,000-year-old volume (some of which was written as much as 3,400 years ago) has survived through the centuries and still speaks to current issues with relevance and wisdom.

**S**cientific and prophetic accuracy. While some may assume that the Bible clashes with scientific facts, its message fits remarkably well with modern scientific discoveries; and fulfilled prophecies point to God's superintendence of the production of the Scriptures.

**T**otal unity. The writers of Scripture were a diverse group, but their books don't contradict one another.

That sums up why the Bible can be considered reliable. The word *Bible* comes from the Greek *biblos,* which means "book" (literally, a "roll," or "scroll," since ancient books were rolled onto sticks instead of bound like modern volumes). When we call it the *holy* Bible, we mean it's the Book of books—a volume like no other—the special, unique, verbal message of God in a permanent, written form.

## Just a Matter of Interpretation?

But Ben voiced a common frustration many people feel about the Bible, when he complained, "If you get ten different people to read the Bible, you might come out with ten different versions. Even though they're reading the same words, they interpret them in an entirely different way." Many skeptics are quick to dismiss the Bible by saying, "It's all a matter of personal interpretation."

In one sense, it *is* a matter of interpretation, for we must carefully apply our minds to the task when we study the Bible. (If this were not the case, non-Christians would have another reason to argue that Christian faith is intellectually unacceptable.) But it's unfair to conclude that Scripture is impossible to understand. Actually, biblical interpretation (also known as hermeneutics) is a highly developed discipline—too broad to examine thoroughly here. But let me offer some basic suggestions as a starting point.

## Focus on what you *can* understand

Bible study is a growth process. I've been married to my wife, Candy, since 1975. I know her a lot better now than I used to; years from now, I'll know her better still. It's much the same as we get acquainted with God. Be inquisitive. Be patient. There are plenty of difficult passages in the Bible, and equally honest believers sometimes disagree about their meanings. But the basic gospel and the foundational moral teachings of the Bible are quite clear.

> Most people are bothered by those passages of Scripture they do not understand, but the passages that bother me are those I do understand.[17]
>
> Mark Twain

## Ask God to help you

Even the Bible itself acknowledges that some of its writings are "hard to understand" (2 Peter 3:15, 16). But the Bible isn't written in some sort of secret code; it's written in human language, and we can grasp its meaning if we study it according to ordinary rules of grammar and logic. God wants to give us wisdom and help us understand his will. That's why he gave us the Bible in the first place (2 Timothy 3:14-17; James 1:5).

## Study the Bible with an open mind

As much as possible, we need to lay aside our preconceived ideas and take a fresh, unbiased look at the Scriptures. Don't read the Bible through colored glasses. Denominational or cultural biases make Bible students look for "proof texts" for their favorite theological causes or political agendas instead of discerning the whole counsel of God. Someone who doesn't think miracles are possible will explain away historical records of miraculous events without giving them a fair examination. As medical doctor Charles Webster points out, "If someone has already decided that one plus one doesn't equal two, then he will never agree that one hundred plus one hundred equals two hundred."

## Let the Bible speak for itself

Correct interpretation of the Scripture requires exegesis, deriving the meaning of Scripture out of (*ex*) the text itself—not eisegesis, reading your own meaning into (*eis*) the text. "The Bible is its own best interpreter," someone has said. Often a question raised in one section of Scripture will be answered by other passages that deal with the same subject.

## Use common sense

Keep Bible verses in context. Note who is speaking, as well as when, where, and why. Use a Bible dictionary, Bible encyclopedia, concordance, or some other reference tool to make sure you know the correct meanings of words. Study biblical events in their historical context. For example, it makes a big difference whether a principle was given under the old covenant of the Jews or the new covenant initiated by Jesus Christ.

And pay attention to the literary form. Is the text meant to be literal or figurative? Is it poetry or prose? Is it a personal letter, a legal document, a proverb, a parable, or a prophecy? These are weighty issues, but they're not impossible to handle if we use common sense and some good Bible study tools.

## Focus on the Bible's main theme

God's Word speaks with spiritual power (1 Thessalonians 2:13; Hebrews 4:12; James 1:18; 1 Peter 1:23-25), but it's not merely a rule book. It's a message about God's redeeming love and his plan for our salvation. It's a living message about the living Christ who died for our sins and rose from the dead. Jesus himself is the heart of the Bible's message (Luke 24:44-47; 1 Corinthians 15:1-4). When you read the Bible, make sure you don't miss the good news!

## Apply it to your life

Once you grasp that a biblical passage is meant for you to obey, don't hesitate to put it into action. Be a doer of God's Word, not just a hearer (James 1:22, 23).

If we follow basic principles like these, we won't cause division and confusion as we seek to interpret the Bible and explain it to others. Rather, the Bible will give us encouragement and hope. The apostle Paul urged Christians to pray, "May the God who gives endurance and encouragement give you a spirit of unity among yourselves as you follow Christ Jesus, so that with one heart and mouth you may glorify the God and Father of our Lord Jesus Christ" (Romans 15:5, 6).

## Not an "Imaginary Mate"

"What would it take for you to believe?" a friend asked Ben.

"Factual proof and evidence," he responded. "If somebody actually has facts and evidence to support what he's saying, then you can't really argue with that."

But there's more to the story. A few years ago, Ben was almost killed in a car accident. His car was hit broadside by another car, and emergency workers had to cut Ben out of his vehicle. For two years he was out of work while he recuperated from his injuries and learned how to walk and talk again. He had been an apprentice cabinetmaker with only one year left in his apprenticeship, but after the accident he had to give up that career and support himself in a less satisfying job.

"I feel frustrated with God," Ben said. "If God is there, why doesn't he answer me, talk to me, show himself? In a time of desperation, I prayed to him, but nothing happened and things kept turning out wrong. It felt like I was talking to an imaginary mate."

Honest questioners like Ben need all the facts we can give them about the Bible. But they also need us to be real "mates"—real friends—as we patiently introduce them to the God who cares. The Bible is a letter from a loving Father, a letter inviting us home and guiding us until we get there.

You can see some beautiful stars in Australia—different ones than you see in the northern hemisphere. It's called the Land of the Southern Cross because one constellation looks like a cross shining brightly in the sky.

Wherever Ben is tonight, I hope he's looking up.

# Honest Questions for Personal Reflection

1. If you were telling a person like Ben why you believe the Bible is God's Word, how would you begin your explanation?

2. Do you think Ben's painful experience with his auto accident might have something to do with his unwillingness to believe the Bible? Why or why not?

3. Which kind of evidence is more compelling to you—fulfilled biblical prophecies (p. 39) or scientific facts included in the Bible (p. 42)? Why?

# Honest Questions for Group Discussion

### Relate

1. Tell the group about one of the following (or more, if time allows):

• the best book you ever read (and why you enjoyed it)
• a book you loved reading when you were a child (and why you enjoyed it)
• a book other people enjoy, but you don't (and why you don't)

2. Ask each member of the group to complete one of the following statements:

A. "My favorite book of the Bible is _____
   because _____ ."

B. "Without the Bible, my life would be different because
   _____ ."

C. "I believe the Bible is God's Word because _____
   _____ ."

D. "I have a lot of questions about the Bible because _____
   _____ ."

3. Each group member will need an index card and a pencil. Each person has three minutes to write on the card a favorite Bible verse reference (for example, "John 3:16") and a sentence or two explaining why this verse has been helpful to him or her. Each person should insert the card into his Bible at the appropriate page and hand it to the person on his right. Then take turns reading everyone's favorite verses and words of explanation.

## Reflect

4. The CHRIST acrostic (p. 43) summarized some of the reasons Christians believe in the reliability of Scripture. What do you think about those points? The acrostic reminds us that Christ himself is the central character of the Bible. Read Luke 24:44-47 and John 17:17. What was Christ's view of Scripture? Why is this important?

5. Ben complained, "If you get ten different people to read the Bible, you might come out with ten different versions." But Christians believe God gave us the Bible so we can know and understand his will. Check any of the following that would help you understand the Bible's message more clearly. Then explain your choices to the group:

____ a translation of the Bible that speaks my language

____ a knowledgeable teacher who can explain confusing passages

____ greater unity among Christians who read the same book but come to different conclusions

____ other:

6. What makes the Bible difficult for you to understand? What helps you understand it better? Share with the group what Bible study tools (reference books, magazines, websites) have helped you the most in your study of God's Word.

## Respond

7. Willing to try some homework? Before the next group meeting, select and read one of the following books of the Bible and come prepared to tell the group your reaction to it:

- The book of James is a short, practical book about Christian living. Estimated reading time: thirty minutes.
- The Gospel of Luke is a physician's description of the historical life of Jesus Christ. Estimated reading time: two hours.
- The Gospel of John is an eyewitness account of Jesus' life and teaching written by one of the twelve apostles. Estimated reading time: two hours.
- The book of Acts is an introduction to the history of the early Christian church. Estimated reading time: two hours.

8. Offer a prayer of praise and thank God for revealing himself through the written Word. See Psalm 119:9-16 for ideas.

# Resources for Further Study

*Discovering God's Story: Fully Illustrated Bible Handbook in Chronological Order* by Jim Eichenberger (Cincinnati: Standard Publishing, 2010). This unique presentation, featuring classic Bible art, reveals how individual Bible stories fit together as one continuous saga.

*Halley's Bible Handbook* by Henry H. Halley (Grand Rapids, MI: Zondervan, revised edition for *NIV*, 2000). First published in the 1920s and long considered a Bible student's first must-have Bible study resource.

Prove the Bible, http://www.provethebible.net

*Solid: The Authority of God's Word* by Jack Cottrell (Eugene, OR: Wipf and Stock, 2002) is a clear and concise little gem.

*The Historical Jesus: Ancient Evidence for the Life of Christ* by Gary Habermas (Joplin, MO: College Press, 1996)

*The Historical Reliability of the Gospels* by Craig Blomberg (Downers Grove, IL: IVP Academic, second edition 2007)

*The New Evidence That Demands a Verdict* by Josh McDowell (Nashville, TN: Thomas Nelson, 1999) and *The Book of Books* by William R. Kimball (Joplin, MO: College Press, 1986) both have chapters that further discuss the uniqueness of the Bible.

*The New Testament Documents: Are They Reliable?* by F. F. Bruce (Grand Rapids, MI: Wm. B. Eerdmans Publishing Company, 2003)

*The Old Testament Documents: Are They Reliable & Relevant?* by Walter C. Kaiser Jr. (Downers Grove, IL: IVP Academic, 2001)

*The New Unger's Bible Dictionary* by Merrill Unger (Chicago: Moody Publishers, revised edition 2006) and *Zondervan's Pictorial Bible Dictionary* by Merrill C. Tenney and J. D. Douglas (Grand Rapids, MI: Zondervan, 1999) are two popular Bible dictionaries.

## Chapter 3

# Who Is God Anyway?

**If . . . you seek the Lᴏʀᴅ your God, you will find him if you look for him with all your heart and with all your soul.**

Moses (Deuteronomy 4:29)

"I'm pretty good at generating questions," Pat[1] said, grinning. "If I start to offend you or if you think I'm getting too heated, tell me right away, OK?"

Then I told her I was writing a book filled with honest questions people ask about faith. Her reaction was immediate and enthusiastic. "Religion is one of my primary interests," she said, smiling thoughtfully, "but I'm one who needs to look at things in her own way and draw her own conclusions. Ideas have to ring true in my gut as well as pass the head test before I can sign on to them."

Then she was quick to insist, "I'm not looking to be converted to anything. What I'm looking for is the truth. I probably won't find it until I'm dead, but that's OK."

## The Big Fuzzy White Thing

A self-described "computer geek" and "fiendish gardener," Pat is married to a chemist who frequently surveys her collection of salvaged computer hardware and sighs, "How many more of these are you going to bring home?" They have no children, just "an extremely spoiled and rather obese yellow Labrador retriever."

"I was a biology major in college—in the pre-med program," she said, "but I didn't have the money or the intestinal fortitude to go through that much school. Biology still interests me though."

I found Pat to be interested in spirituality but cautious about opening up what she calls the Religion Zone. As she put it, "I'm not crazy about religious discussions that generate more heat than light, and I find the use of any religion as a means to kill, maim, discriminate, or generally behave like an idiot particularly abhorrent!"

Perhaps I registered some surprise, because she added, "I have some nasty baggage regarding the religious right. When my sister first told me she had become a Christian, I immediately was afraid that she would be out bombing abortion clinics the following day!"

Pat had read "a ton" of religious writing: "bits of the Bible and some assorted Buddhist and New Age writings and *Black Elk Speaks,* the life story of an Oglala Sioux holy man."

Her view of God?

"I've been turned off to the words *God* and *Jesus* because of the bad things people have done while invoking those names," she said. "I tend to refer to God as the Big Fuzzy White Thing (BFWT), because that term doesn't have the baggage, and it's more gender neutral. That's more how I think of him/her/it."

## Pieces of the Truth

"I don't have many cast-in-concrete beliefs," said Pat. "There are really only two it will take a lot to get me to relinquish."

One of those is her belief in reincarnation. "I have no proof," she said, "but it makes a lot of sense. Why base judgment of a person for all eternity on one lifetime, when they might have been plunked down in rotten circumstances and died young? If I were designing a universe, I'd rotate beings through all sorts of different circumstances so that they would learn more."

Pat's other main belief is "the feeling that all religions have a piece of the truth but they don't see the whole picture. Isn't there a tale about an elephant behind a curtain with people reaching through, grabbing different parts of it and judging what animal it is, based on what piece they are holding onto? That's sort of how I feel."

Pat had other questions too. "The necessity of Jesus. Why isn't a relationship with the BFWT enough? What is the point of Jesus? As an example? teacher? savior? lunatic? None of the above?"

She questioned "the exclusivity of Christianity," saying, "If you think of God as a room, Christians believe there is only one door into the room and Christianity is it. I'm not saying Christianity isn't a door," she was quick to point out. "I just don't understand why it's the *only* one. And I won't accept something simply because the Bible says it."

## Let's Talk About It

Pat has spent a considerable time thinking about all this, and there's a lot at stake in the way we deal with the issues. If there really is a God who cares about us—who created us, who answers prayer, who offers hope—it only makes sense to get acquainted with him and find out what he expects of us.

"Some people see no value in a journey unless they reach a destination," said Pat. "I'm the opposite. I think the journey is often more interesting than the destination."

Like others in a postmodern world, Pat has sampled a wide variety of religions but is unwilling to commit firmly to any of them. She is uncomfortable with Christianity because it seems too exclusive, and she's especially turned off by the religious right. She wants a faith that makes sense, yet she admits she believes in reincarnation even though there's no proof for it. To further complicate matters, she is unsure about the trustworthiness of the Bible; so if we try to use the Bible to defend our faith, she may accuse us of circular reasoning, or she may not listen at all.

Pat refers to God as the BFWT and cringes at the very names of God and Jesus. If we can help her understand who God is, then we'll be able to clear up some of her other concerns as well.

## Getting Started

With someone like Pat who already has her defenses up, you can't come across as preachy or manipulative. As we began our conversation, I complimented her honesty and thanked her for opening the door to the Religion Zone.

Even though she plainly disagreed with my Christian beliefs, she said she wasn't looking for a quarrel. But I pointed out, "Even a heated argument isn't all bad, because at least it shows that people care deeply about the topic they're discussing." I continued: "I have trouble understanding the 'who cares' attitude so many people seem to have about matters of faith. To me, issues like the existence of God and the reliability of the Bible are too important to ignore. I don't want to fritter away my life on 'matters that don't matter' if there really is a God who answers prayer and gives purpose to life. And if Christian faith is true, as I believe, then it will stand up in the give-and-take of serious examination. Jesus never avoided the hard questions, nor should we."

I also thought it wise to talk with Pat about the word *religion*. "You might be surprised to learn," I said, "that the word rarely appears in the Bible. And when it does, the Scripture simply says, 'If anyone considers himself religious and yet does not keep a tight rein on his tongue, he deceives himself and his religion is worthless.

Before one can say that the world is without a God, he must first have become thoroughly conversant with the whole world. He must have searched through the universe of suns and stars, as well as the history of all ages; he must have wandered through the whole realm of space and time in order to be able to assert with truth, "Nowhere has a trace of God been found!" . . . In short, to be able to affirm authoritatively that no God exists, a man must be omniscient and omnipresent, that is, he himself must be God; and then after all there would be one.[2]

Theodor Christlieb

Religion that God our Father accepts as pure and faultless is this: to look after orphans and widows in their distress and to keep oneself from being polluted by the world' (James 1:26, 27). Isn't that an interesting definition of 'pure and faultless' religion? Watch our words. Take care of parentless children and widows. Avoid hypocrisy and things that pollute our souls. I'm not sure a lot of people would define *religion* like that. But if believers put that kind of faith into practice, you wouldn't have to worry about so-called Christians who use religion as an excuse to harm others."

I explained, "I'm a Christian. A believer in the God of the Bible. A follower of Christ. I don't have a halo over my head. I don't sit in a corner praying twenty-four hours a day, and I don't try to do 'good works' so God or others will be impressed with me. I'm a normal guy with a mortgage and a car payment. But I also believe that Jesus is who he claimed to be, that the Bible is true, and that there's hope for me when I die. If you want to call that religion, OK. But I'd rather just talk about faith. To me, following Christ is simply a way of life, not a religion I practice."

That made sense to Pat.

As we began our actual discussion, I asked her, "If you don't mind my asking, what exactly is your 'baggage' from the 'religious right'?"

She had a lot to say. For example, she'd had a bad experience as a fourteen-year-old student in a church's confirmation class. The minister said she shouldn't be confirmed because she had too many questions. But to please her parents, she went ahead and gave "the right answers" so she could be confirmed. Instead of finding the answers she needed, she learned to repress her questions and be suspicious of anything Christian.

Pat had said, "The journey is often more interesting than the destination." I challenged her to look at that a different way.

"What if the point of life is to appreciate *both*?" I ventured. "What if God created us with the capacity to enjoy the journey while, at the same time, there really is a destination or goal he has in mind for us? What if he gave us a road map to guide us? And better yet, what if God himself wants to accompany us on the journey?"

## Getting to Know God

As my dialogue with Pat continued, I took some steps to help her understand what I believe about God and why I believe it. If you know someone like Pat, perhaps these ideas will help you as well.

## Ask your friend to describe the God in whom she does not believe

Like Pat, many people hold a distorted, unbiblical concept of God. It can help if you explain that you don't believe in that kind of god either.

Some folks think of God as sort of a cosmic Dirty Harry—a harsh judge just waiting for a chance to say "Go ahead, make my day." To others, he's the divine version of a cuddly, American sitcom dad—often humorous, forgiving . . . but not someone to fear. Still others see him as the Force, Star Wars style. In his book *Your God Is Too Small*, J. B. Phillips pointed out that many people believe in a divine being who is little more than a "parental hangover," a "pale Galilean," a "God-in-a-box," or some other inadequate god.[3]

Pat thinks of God as the Big Fuzzy White Thing. Not exactly a biblical designation for the Almighty, but at least it's a place to start. And we need to start where our friends are, not where we'd like them to be.

## Tell your friend about the God in whom you believe

We can't explain everything about God. If we could comprehend him fully, he wouldn't be God. To fit all knowledge about the infinite God into our finite brains would be like trying to fit the ocean into a teacup. Nevertheless, we do know much about God because he has revealed himself to us through the world he created; through the Word he inspired; and most of all, through his Son Jesus Christ (Hebrews 1:1-4). We need to understand God in biblical terms. The God described in the Bible is far more than the BFWT.

Here are ten personal qualities of God described in Scripture.[4]

*1. Alive, and the giver of life.* God is the "living God" (Matthew 16:16; 1 Timothy 4:10; Hebrews 10:31). He's not a lifeless idol but a divine being who always has been alive and always will be alive.

2. *Spirituality and personality.* "God is spirit," Jesus said (John 4:24), not an impersonal force. He is self-conscious, rational, intelligent, thoughtful, and capable of entering into loving relationships. He is the great "I AM" (Exodus 3:14).

3. *All-knowing and all-powerful.* He knows every detail of our lives (Psalm 139:1-6; Hebrews 4:13), and "with God all things are possible" (Matthew 19:26). That is, he has unlimited power to do all things that are consistent with his nature and purpose (Psalm 115:3; Jeremiah 32:17). We require several hours of sleep every night—a consistent reminder of our human weakness and mortality—but God never runs out of energy (see Psalm 121:3, 4).

4. *Eternal and ever-present.* We live by the clock and measure time in years, months, days, and hours; God has no beginning or end. He was there when time began (Genesis 1:1), and he is immortal (1 Timothy 6:15, 16; Jude 25). He's "the Alpha and the Omega, the First and the Last, the Beginning and the End" (Revelation 22:13). He cannot be limited by space, for he created space (Deuteronomy 10:14), and there's no place we can go to escape from his awareness (Psalm 139:7-10; Jeremiah 23:23, 24).

5. *Holy, holy, holy.* He is set apart, distinct, different from all else. Heavenly angels stand in awe of his glory (Psalm 99:5; Isaiah 6:3; Revelation 4:8). He is separate from all sin and impurity (Habakkuk 1:13; 1 Peter 1:14-16).

6. *Truthful and faithful.* He never lies. It's his nature to be truthful (Titus 1:2; Hebrews 6:18). God keeps his promises. We can rely on him completely (Lamentations 3:22, 23; Hebrews 10:23).

7. *Righteous and just.* Always fair and good, he is the perfect standard of all that is right (Deuteronomy 32:3, 4; Daniel 4:37; Psalm 96:13). "God is light; in him there is no darkness at all" (1 John 1:5).

8. *Jealous and angry.* God's jealousy is not spiteful ill will or envy. It's a protective jealousy—the kind of earnest concern a devoted husband rightly feels for his wife, or the vigilant way a loving father watches out for anyone who would harm his children (see 2 Corinthians 11:2, 3). God

isn't a passive, mild-mannered deity. He possesses intense concern for the welfare of his people (Exodus 20:5, 6; 34:14). His jealousy is a righteous anger toward sin—the natural reaction of his holy nature against all that is hurtful and wrong (Romans 1:18; 2:6-10; Revelation 20:7-15). God is justly jealous when we give our attention, loyalty, and reverence to someone or something besides him. He alone is God (Isaiah 45:6, 22).

*9. Loving and gracious.* God always acts with intelligent goodwill toward the objects of his love. So generous is his giving, so profound his personal sacrifices, the Bible even says that "God is love" (1 John 4:8-11; see also John 3:16; Romans 5:5; 2 Corinthians 13:11-14; Titus 3:4-7). Through Christ, he graciously gives us far more than we deserve and mercifully spares us from punishments we *do* deserve (Ephesians 2:1-10; 1 Timothy 1:16; 1 Peter 5:10).

*10. Unchanging.* God is not fickle or unreliable. He is steadfast and consistent (Malachi 3:6; James 1:17).

## Explain why you believe the God described in the Bible exists

Why do you believe in God? Can you put your reasons into words? Philosophers have offered complicated answers, but people like Pat want answers that "ring true" on a gut level and "pass the head test."

> This would be a sad epitaph for modern science: It revealed wonders but was numb to wonder.[5]
> Michael Gerson

I started with a personal testimony: "I understand why you might question God. But to me, he's inescapable, even when I try to run from him. Even in my lowest times of doubt and discouragement, my mind can't completely deny him. My emotions cry out for him. My strength fails without him. Jesus said that the greatest commandment is to love God with all our heart, soul, mind, and strength. This makes sense to me, because when I'm honest, I realize every part of my being longs for relationship with my Creator."

Then I told her, "At the risk of oversimplifying a complex subject, here are three reasons I believe the God revealed in Scripture is the true and living God."

1. *The universe requires a creator.* "In the beginning God created the heavens and the earth" (Genesis 1:1). He preceded all creation, he planned it, he has a purpose for it, he put it all together by his power. Whether you look through a telescope or through a microscope, at the orbits of the planets or at the wings of a hummingbird, you can see order and complexity in nature that point to the hand of God.

Scientist John Haldane once asked theologian Ronald Knox, "In a universe containing millions of planets, is it not inevitable that life should appear on at least one of them?"

"Sir," replied Knox, "if Scotland Yard found a body in your cabin trunk, would you tell them: 'There are millions of trunks in the world; surely one of them must contain a body'? I think they would still want to know who put it there."[6]

Because of Pat's interest in biology, this argument makes sense to her. "Nature," someone has said, "is God's Braille to a blind world." The true God must be higher than his creation; so Christians can't accept pantheism (the idea that everything is God) or panentheism (the idea that everything is *in* God) or any kind of idolatry that reduces God to a part of nature itself (see Romans 1:18-20).

2. *Life requires a designer*—especially human life. A single molecule of human DNA contains roughly the same amount of information as a volume of an encyclopedia. A single living cell functions like a tiny factory. Your human body contains a highly complicated computer (brain), pump (heart), furnace (stomach), camera (eye), musical instrument (ear), communication network (nerves) . . . all designed to move around on a flexible but sturdy structural framework (bones), under a protective covering (skin) that allows perspiration to escape when you exercise but keeps water from pouring into your body when you bathe or swim.

Cause and effect is a matter of common sense. A story requires an author. A song requires a composer. A painting requires an artist. A computer code requires a programmer. A law code requires a lawgiver. A meal requires a cook. A child requires a parent. Doesn't the universe require a designer?

Even if an evolutionary theory could satisfactorily explain (and none has) how we humans developed such amazing bodies through purely natural means, it would only have scratched the surface of the problem. Where did we get the spiritual part of our being? How did we develop what Christian apologist Francis Schaeffer used to call our "unique mannishness"?[7] Where did we get our minds, wills, morals, emotions, and aspirations? How did we even come up with the idea of God, if we are not made in his image? Don't we instinctively recognize that we are "fearfully and wonderfully made" (Psalm 139:13, 14) and that God has "set eternity in the hearts of men" (Ecclesiastes 3:11)?

When Pat suggested that "all religions have a piece of the truth," I told her, "I agree with you in one sense. I think everyone is born with an intuitive awareness that God exists. We have a moral law within us. Even the Bible acknowledges this (Romans 2:14, 15, for example). We all have an innate longing to know God because we're made in God's image."

"I like that 'moral law within' statement," Pat agreed. "I tend to run things past an internal compass in my gut when I'm not sure what's right."

*3. The Bible requires a revealer.* We need to be careful not to engage in circular reasoning ("I believe in God because the Bible says so, and I believe the Bible because God revealed it.") But it's not circular reasoning to say something like this:

> There's sufficient reason to believe God exists, even if we didn't have the Bible. But without the Bible, how could we know what God expects of us? How could we know about his grace and his plan for our salvation? If God exists, it's reasonable to think he would communicate with creatures made in his image. The Bible has proved reliable in countless areas (like historical details) where we can check its accuracy [see my answer to Ben in chapter 2], so it's reasonable to trust its accuracy in areas we can't check.

The Bible's human authors wrote it with assistance from God (see 2 Timothy 3:16, 17; 2 Peter 1:20, 21). If Pat disagrees with this conclusion, she must explain how a magnificent book like the Bible could be produced, without any divine help, by ordinary people.

## Challenge your friend to ponder the consequences of her worldview

Non-Christians often put Christians on the defensive. But sometimes we need to turn the tables and compel our unbelieving friends to face the consequences of their beliefs. Here are some questions we can ask:

1. *"If God is nothing but the Big Fuzzy White Thing, what does that make* you?" Are you simply a grown-up germ that emerged from the slime through eons of evolution? Apart from the biblical view that we are created in the image of God, is there really any reference point for human dignity?

2. *"Are your views logical or simply wishful thinking?"* I asked Pat, "Aren't you making a big leap of faith to believe in reincarnation simply because it seems right to you, even though you admit there's no proof for it?"

3. *"Do you have any hope of life after death?"* Christians believe in eternal life because we hold that Jesus really rose from the dead. If you don't accept his resurrection, do you have any reasonable basis for hope?

4. *"Do you have positive convictions to believe in, or are you mainly just reacting against traditional views of God you find difficult to accept?"* There is something fundamentally negative about being an atheist (or an agnostic). Does it make sense to build your whole philosophy of life on something you deny, something you *don't* believe in? To define yourself by something you're *not*? If you define yourself to me by saying, "I'm an atheist" ("I'm a person who doesn't believe in God"), then would I define myself to you by saying, "I'm an aBuddhist" ("I'm a person who doesn't believe in Buddha")? No! I'd rather not describe my beliefs primarily in reference to what I *don't* believe.

What I *am* is a follower of Jesus, a willing servant of the Most High God. That's ennobling, positive, uplifting.

5. *"Do you have real peace of mind?"* This little slogan is trite but true: "No God, no peace. Know God, know peace." As Blaise Pascal said, "There is a God-shaped vacuum in the heart of every man, which cannot be filled by any created thing, but only by God, the Creator, made known through Jesus."[8]

## Focus the Discussion on Jesus Christ

In my conversations with Pat, the ultimate question I wanted her to consider was simply, "Who is Jesus Christ?" A Christian's strongest argument for the existence of God is what I call the Jesus Argument. If Jesus is who he claimed to be, then we not only know there is a God; we also know what God is like by looking at Jesus.

How can we be sure God isn't just the BFWT? Because two thousand years ago he came to earth in the person called Jesus of Nazareth.

Philip, one of Jesus' disciples, spoke for honest questioners everywhere when he said, "Lord, show us the Father and that will be enough for us."

Jesus said in response, "Don't you know me, Philip, even after I have been among you such a long time? Anyone who has seen me has seen the Father. How can you say, 'Show us the Father'?" (John 14:8, 9).

The God of the Bible isn't a fluffy, mystical power; he is the Word who "became flesh and made his dwelling among us." And while "no one has ever seen God," God's Son "has made him known," or explained him to us (John 1:14, 18). The apostle Peter wrote of Jesus, "Through him you believe in God, who raised him from the dead and glorified him" (1 Peter 1:21).

Jesus of Nazareth claimed attributes, powers, and honors that belong only to God. His followers believed him to be God. Speaking of Jesus, John wrote, "The Word was God" (John 1:1). Paul said, "In Christ all the fullness of the Deity lives in bodily form" (Colossians 2:9). The doubter Thomas eventually called Jesus "my Lord and my God" (John 20:28).

Statements like those appear even more impressive when you recall that Jesus' original disciples were Jewish monotheists who understood that it would be blasphemy for a mere man to claim to be God.[9]

As C. S. Lewis pointed out in *Mere Christianity*,

> A man who was merely a man and said the sort of things Jesus said would not be a great moral teacher. He would either be a lunatic—on a level with the man who says he is a poached egg—or else he would be the Devil of Hell. You must make your choice. Either this man was, and is, the Son of God: or else a madman or something worse. You can shut Him up for a fool, you can spit at Him and kill Him as a demon; or you can fall at His feet and call Him Lord and God. But let us not come with any patronising nonsense about His being a great human teacher. He has not left that open to us.[10]

## Keep the Discussion Going

I continued my dialogue with Pat for months, but she remained unconvinced. Who knows? Maybe I've planted a gospel seed someone else will water. Perhaps in time, Pat will find her heart softening to the Word of God.

Don't be discouraged just because someone rejects your Christian testimony at first. If you had lived in the first century, would you have thought there was any chance that Saul of Tarsus, the church's arch-enemy, would eventually become a Christian? If you noticed how so many Jewish leaders opposed the gospel, would you have expected that eventually a large number of priests would be obedient to the faith? But that's exactly what happened (Acts 6:7).

Never underestimate the gospel. "It is the power of God for the salvation of everyone who believes" (Romans 1:16). Like a sharp sword, God's "living and active" Word "penetrates even to dividing soul and spirit, joints and marrow; it judges the thoughts and attitudes of the heart" (Hebrews 4:12). God says, "My word . . . will not return to me empty, but will accomplish what I desire and achieve the purpose for which I sent it" (Isaiah 55:11).

My friend Shawn serves on the staff of a church in the Midwest. Alexis, a woman in her late twenties, entered the church office one day.[11] She had not been inside a church since her childhood, but on this day she wanted to meet with a minister. Her first words to Shawn were, "I don't believe there's a God."

Alexis didn't believe in God because of evolution ("Evolution has been scientifically proven to be true and just doesn't mesh with Christianity") and because of painful experiences she had endured in her life (especially the death of her mother when she was very young). But she wasn't at peace with her decision to reject God. She wanted a minister to have one chance at talking her out of her disbelief, because she needed to know for sure. Shawn spoke with Alexis for a while and then introduced her to his wife. They struck up a friendship and eventually studied the Bible together.

"Every Monday," Shawn explained, "I would receive a list from Alexis with questions about the Sunday sermon or other questions she was coming up with from her own reading of Scripture. None of her questions were especially difficult to answer but were important because they began linking the truth of Scripture to the reality of her life."

Shawn continued, "Almost exactly a year after Alexis walked into the church office, I had the honor of baptizing her into a relationship with Jesus Christ. Almost another year later to the day, I had the privilege of baptizing her husband."

Looking back on his experience with Alexis, Shawn remarked, "Few things in life bring me more joy than meeting someone who is truly willing not only to ask the big questions about God but also to seek the answers."

# Honest Questions for Personal Reflection

1. On a scale of 0 (not even sure God exists) to 10 (strong faith in God), where would you rate your relationship with God? Put an X through the number where your faith was five years ago. Circle where your faith is now. What do you think is responsible for any change?

0    1    2    3    4    5    6    7    8    9    10

2. What are your impressions of Pat, the woman described in this chapter? What do you like about her? Do you think you'd enjoy talking about your faith with someone like her? Why or why not?

# Honest Questions for Group Discussion

**Relate**

1. When it comes to getting directions, confess which of the following statements best describes you?

____ I'm usually too stubborn to ask for directions. I'd rather find my own way.

____ I'm terrible at finding my own way. If I had been Lewis and Clark's guide, they'd still be wandering somewhere in the Rocky Mountains!

____ I'm willing to ask for directions, but they'd better be accurate!

____ I avoid traveling to new places, so I never need directions.

____ I'd much rather ask directions than fumble around by myself.

2. Imagine that someone has asked you, "Why do you believe in God? If you had only one minute to answer, what would you say to point the person to God?

## Reflect

3. Page 60 gave three basic reasons why it makes sense to believe that the God revealed in Scripture exists. Which of those reasons do you think is most likely to help convince a skeptic about the reality of God? What reasons would you add to the list?

4. Jesus said, "Anyone who has seen me has seen the Father" (John 14:9). Make a list of some facts we know about God that we wouldn't understand if Jesus had never come to earth.

5. Even a person who is struggling to know God usually has some ideas about the kind of deity he or she *doesn't* believe in. What kind of god are you pretty sure you don't believe in? Why?

## Respond

6. Do you know someone like Pat who struggles to believe in God? What could you say or do that might help your friend take a step closer to faith? Make a plan toward having such a conversation.

7. Focus your closing prayer time on these thoughts found in Psalm 139:

- Praise God for his intimate concern about every detail of our lives (vv. 1-6).
- Praise God for his consistent presence with us no matter where we go (vv. 7-10).
- Praise God for giving us life and creating us to fulfill an important purpose (vv. 13-16).
- Praise God for revealing his "precious" thoughts to us through the Bible (vv. 17, 18).
- Ask God to search our hearts and to lead us in his ways, especially as we reach out to others who don't know him (vv. 23, 24).

# Resources for Further Study

*Can Man Live Without God?* by Ravi Zacharias (Nashville, TN: Thomas Nelson, 2004)

*Evidence for God: 50 Arguments for Faith from the Bible, History, Philosophy, and Science,* William A. Dembski and Mike Licona, editors (Grand Rapids, MI: Baker Books, 2010)

*God Is Great, God Is Good: Why Believing in God Is Reasonable and Responsible,* William Lane Craig and Chad Meister, editors (Downers Grove, IL: InterVarsity Press, 2009)

*Is God a Moral Monster? Making Sense of the Old Testament God* by Paul Copan (Grand Rapids, MI: Baker Books, 2011)

*Knowing God* by J. I. Packer (Downers Grove, IL: InterVarsity, 1977)

*The Reason for God: Belief in an Age of Skepticism* by Timothy Keller (New York: Dutton / Penguin, 2008)

*The God You're Looking For* by Bill Hybels (Nashville, TN: Thomas Nelson, 1997)

*What the Bible Says About God the Creator; What the Bible Says About God the Ruler; What the Bible Says About God the Redeemer.* All in Jack Cottrell's The Doctrine of God series (Eugene, OR: Wipf & Stock Publishers, 2001). In-depth but approachable.

## Chapter 4

# How Should I Handle My Doubts?

**Faith is taking the first step even when you don't see the whole staircase.** **Martin Luther King Jr.**

In my role as president of Cincinnati Christian University, I usually enjoy hearing our alumni share their memories about the good old days they spent on campus. Larry Carter caught me off guard though.[1] My heart sank when he looked me in the eye and exclaimed, "Dave, I lost my faith at Cincinnati Christian University!"

Here's the rest of the story. While Larry was enrolled back in the 1970s, he started hanging out with guys from another local university who influenced him in a negative way and pulled him away from the Lord. His doubts grew until finally one day he went into the office of a CCU philosophy professor and blurted out, "I have lost my faith!"

Without hesitation, the professor exclaimed, "Praise the Lord!"

Larry wondered if the fellow had lost his mind, but as they continued to talk, the wise professor explained, "Larry, you haven't lost *your* faith. You've lost your *parents'* faith. Now it's time to find a faith of your own."

Larry told me, "That's when my own faith really began to take root and grow."

Years later he is a firm believer in Christ, serving as president of Great Lakes Christian College in Lansing, Michigan. He is deeply grateful for what he learned from his professors at CCU, because they didn't tear down his faith; they built it up.

I had a memorable experience similar to Larry's when I was in Bible college and listening to my esteemed professor, Mr. Gill, lecture about the life of Christ. He came to Matthew 11:2, 3 that says, "When John heard in prison what Christ was doing, he sent his disciples to ask him 'Are you the one who was to come, or should we expect someone else?'"

Confused, I raised my hand to ask a question. "Mr. Gill, I've never noticed this passage before," I said, "and to tell you the truth, it bothers me. How could John the Baptist ask Jesus if he was 'the one who was to come'? John had baptized Jesus. He had called Jesus the Lamb of God who takes away the sin of the world. He had heard God's voice speak from Heaven and affirm that Jesus is his beloved Son. He had seen the Holy Spirit come down like a dove as a sign of God's approval. So how could John ask if Jesus was really the Messiah?"

Mr. Gill was a kind and godly man, but he could be very intimidating when he wanted to be—and this was one of those moments. Glaring at me intensely, he said, "Mr. Faust [*that was part of the intimidation—when he really wanted to drive home a point, he called you by your last name*], did you believe in Jesus when you first became a Christian?"

"Of . . . of course," I stammered.

Continuing his interrogation while the other students looked on, he asked, "Have you ever had any questions about Jesus since?"

"Well, yes," I said.

The professor's voice began to grow louder. "John the Baptist was in prison when he asked this question of Jesus—and he had been thrown into prison for preaching the truth and rebuking King Herod for committing adultery. Now, if you were thrown into prison for doing the right thing, don't you think you might have a few questions to ask the Lord?"

"Yes," I admitted sheepishly.

Mr. Gill pounded his fist on the lectern and said, "Mr. Faust, if you sometimes have doubts, why can't John have his?" His voice practically thundered: "Let these people in the Bible be real! LET THEM BE REAL!

I have never forgotten the lesson I learned from Mr. Gill that day. The people described in the Bible were real people—and their struggles with faith were just as real as ours, their honest questions just as serious as ours.

## The Problem of Doubt

Doubt is a difficult issue for Christians. As someone has said, "We shouldn't dig up in doubt what we planted in faith." Certainly we don't want to question the trustworthiness of God.

- Jesus told Peter as he sank into the sea, "You of little faith, why did you doubt?" (Matthew 14:31).
- Jesus told his disciples, "If you have faith and do not doubt . . . you can say to this mountain, 'Go, throw yourself into the sea,' and it will be done" (Matthew 21:21).
- Jesus said to Thomas, "Stop doubting and believe"(John 20:27).

Clearly, doubt is not something to be casual about. Yet many of us— even deeply committed believers— do struggle with doubt. Some Christians are reluctant to admit that they have any questions at all, for they see doubt as treason against faith, or even an unpardonable sin.

> Doubt can only be removed by action.[2]
>
> Johann Wolfgang von Goethe

But we can't resolve our doubts unless we identify and face them; and in the process, we will become better equipped to assist our friends who wrestle with doubt.

The stakes are high. Bertrand Russell, a famous opponent of Christianity and author of *Why I Am Not a Christian,* believed in God when he was a boy. During adolescence, he began to doubt his faith but kept his questions secret because he didn't want to upset others by giving voice to his doubts. Years later he recalled that during those formative years he suffered acutely, both from the gradual loss of his faith and from the necessity of keeping his doubts to himself.[3] Bertrand Russell was left with the tragic impression that he dare not even mention his honest questions about faith.

## A Deeper Look at Doubt

The word *doubt* comes from the Latin *dubitare,* which is also where we get our word *dubious.* Its root is a word meaning "two." (Notice the similarity between *doubt* and *double.*) Doubt is double-mindedness, a divided state of mind in which a person wavers between believing and disbelieving. "He who doubts," wrote James, "is like a wave of the sea, blown and tossed by the wind. . . . He is a double-minded man, unstable in all he does" (James 1:6, 8). In English, we say that a doubter is "sitting on the fence." The Chinese have a similar expression; they use the humorous analogy of a person "having a foot in two boats."[4]

Doubts don't necessarily go away simply because you accept Christ. In the Bible, numerous individuals asked honest questions and wrestled with doubt in one form or another.

## Old Testament questioners

Even though you accept the fact of God's existence, you may find yourself wondering at times about the acts of God—why he says what he says and does what he does. For example . . .

*Abraham and Sarah.* When God informed them that they were going to have a baby in their old age, Sarah laughed. (After all, you don't see a lot of ninety-year-old women in the birthing center.) Later, when their son was born, they named the boy Isaac, which means "he laughs" (Genesis 18:9-15; 21:3).

*Moses.* At the burning bush God called Moses to lead his people out of Egyptian bondage, but Moses came up with one excuse after another: "Who am I to do this? What if the people don't believe me? I don't speak very well, Lord, so why don't you send someone else?" (see Exodus 3, 4). As someone has said, Moses' attitude was, "Here am I. Send Aaron!"

*Gideon.* After the Midianites and other groups ransacked his home-land, Gideon found himself threshing wheat in the stifling discomfort of a winepress. God's angel appeared and said, "The LORD is with you, mighty warrior." But if there was anything Gideon didn't feel like right then, it was a mighty warrior. So he answered the angel with an honest question: "But sir, . . . if the LORD is with us, why has all this happened to us? Where are all his wonders that our fathers told us about?" (Judges 6:11-13).

*Job* wondered about the goodness of God and asked, "If I have sinned, what have I done to you, O watcher of men? Why have you made me your target? Have I become a burden to you?" (Job 7:20).

*David* felt abandoned by God and asked, "How long, O LORD? Will you forget me forever? How long will you hide your face from me?" (Psalm 13:1).

*Habakkuk* wondered why God postponed his answers to prayer and sometimes refused to intervene at all. He asked, "How long, O LORD, must I call for help, but you do not listen? Or cry out to you, 'Violence!' but you do not save? Why do you make me look at injustice? Why do you tolerate wrong?" (Habakkuk 1:2, 3).

### New Testament questioners

*Zechariah.* This aging priest found it hard to believe the angel's prom-ise that Elizabeth, Zechariah's wife, would bear a son (Luke 1:18-20).

*Jesus' brothers.* At one point in Jesus' ministry, even James, Jude, and other members of his own family didn't believe in him (John 7:1-5; com-pare Mark 3:21; 6:1-3).

*Martha* confessed her faith in God's power to raise the dead, but she hesitated when Jesus said to open her brother's sealed tomb after four days (John 11:27, 38-40).

*Thomas* is famous for the way he demanded empirical evidence of Jesus' resurrection (John 20:24-29), but he was not really very different from the rest of the apostles, who refused to believe the first reports that Jesus was alive again (Luke 24:9-12).

*Other disciples.* After Jesus' resurrection, in the verse immediately before the Lord's famous Great Commission, Scripture notes that "when they saw him, they worshiped him; but some doubted" even then (Matthew 28:17).

Descartes said, "If you would be a real seeker after truth, it is necessary that at least once in your life you doubt, as far as possible, all things."[5] The fact that the people closest to Jesus still had trouble believing him shows that they were not mindless sheep, blindly following anyone who came along with a tantalizing new message. *Because* they were thinking, reasoning people, the fact that Christ did not act as they expected him to gave them problems. Like us, they wanted God to act as they thought he should, and they found it hard to accept him on his own terms.

## Doubters We're Likely to Encounter

Why do people doubt? For many different reasons. We make a serious mistake if we assume that all doubt is the same and all doubters require the same treatment. Our friends need us to listen respectfully to their honest questions in order to discern the source of their doubt. Let's get to the "heart" of some kinds of doubt.

*Slow of heart.* The two disciples Jesus encountered on the road to Emmaus were "slow of heart" to understand the deeper meaning of what was going on (Luke 24:25). Some people, unfamiliar with the Bible, simply lack the information that could help them believe. A friend told me that when he was growing up, his parents' big, family Bible was little more than a "mystery book" to him. He doubted because he hadn't been informed, and it took a while for him to embrace the gospel.

*Troubled heart* (see John 14:1). Under stress, we may find ourselves perplexed and immobilized by uncertainty and indecision. Even though Jesus' disciples believed in him strongly, they didn't know how to react at first to his strange-sounding predictions about his coming crucifixion (Mark 9:30-32). Troublesome doubts arise even when we are deeply devoted to the Lord. C. S. Lewis wrote about what often happens after a person comes to faith: "I can tell that man what is going to happen to him in the next few weeks. There will come a moment when there is bad news, or he is in trouble, or is living among a lot of other people who do not believe it, and all at once his emotions will rise up and carry out a sort of blitz on his belief. . . . Now Faith, in the sense in which I am here using the word, is the art of holding on to things your reason has once accepted, in spite of your changing moods."[6]

*Faint of heart.* Sometimes doubt results from weariness, from physical or emotional stress. After Elijah's dramatic victory over the prophets of Baal on Mount Carmel, when the Lord had sent fire from Heaven to consume the sacrifice and prove that he alone was God, Elijah ran for his life from the wicked Queen Jezebel. It should have been the prophet's finest hour—a mountaintop experience to savor—but instead he found himself exhausted in the desert, sleeping under a broom tree and asking God to take his life (1 Kings 19:1-5).

> In faith there is enough light for those who want to believe and enough shadows to blind those who don't.[7]
>
> Blaise Pascal

*Fearful heart.* Feelings of personal inadequacy come from focusing on one's own weaknesses rather than the Lord and his strength. It's actually self-doubt—the frightening, almost paralyzing, this-job-is-bigger-than-I-am kind of uneasiness that caused even great men like Moses, Jeremiah, and Paul to hesitate and ask, "Who is equal to such a task?" (2 Corinthians 2:16; see also Exodus 4:10-13; Jeremiah 1:6). If you've ever tried to tackle a task that looked too big to accomplish, you understand the doubt of inadequacy.

*Wounded heart.* This is the result of previous disillusionment—being disappointed by God, feeling frustrated by an unanswered prayer, or being let down by a Christian you trusted. If in the past you have been hurt or felt like your hopes have been dashed by the Lord or by one of his followers, you might choose the security of doubt over the risk of facing further disappointment.

When Jesus appeared to his disciples after rising from the dead, at first "they still did not believe it because of joy and amazement" (Luke 24:41). It seemed too good to be true. Os Guinness points out, "What they were seeing was the one thing in all the world they wanted most. That was precisely the trouble. They wanted it so much that to believe it and then discover it was false would have been profoundly disillusioning."[8]

While it's not necessarily a sin to feel weary, perplexed, or disillusioned, some other forms of doubt plainly cross the line into sin, for they involve willful doubts, doubts we choose. Here are three of those kinds of hearts.

*Stubborn heart.* There is such a thing as stubborn unbelief. Did you ever meet a person who willfully refuses to accept the truth no matter how much evidence you offer? Someone who will never be convinced no matter what you do?

It can be exasperating when you encounter outright spiritual blindness. Jesus was deeply distressed by those who stubbornly refused to believe even after he'd presented them with large amounts of evidence (Matthew 11:20-24; Mark 3:5; 16:14).

*Rebellious heart.* Similarly, there is the doubt of unsubmissiveness—a heart that will agree with Christians in theory but still won't respond in faith and obedience. Scripture has another word for this attitude: *stiff-necked.* What a vivid word picture! When you have a stiff neck, you find it hard to turn and look at things from a different point of view.

In cases like these, the person's intellectual objections serve as little more than a smoke screen. The real problem isn't lack of evidence, but moral stubbornness or rebellion. Some would rather doubt than repent and change their lifestyle. "Men loved darkness instead of light because their deeds were evil" (John 3:19). For others, who live outwardly moral lives, the problem isn't so much a matter of doing evil deeds as it is an unwillingness to submit themselves to God's authority. Remember, even someone like Saul of Tarsus needed the forgiveness found only in Christ, though he had appeared moral on the outside (see Galatians 1:14; Philippians 3:3-6). Likewise, Cornelius prayed and gave generously to help those in need, but this proud soldier still needed to submit himself to the Lord and accept the gospel (Acts 10).

*Divided heart.* Perhaps most frightening is the doubt of complacency. The person remains uncommitted and apathetic—so comfortable with the status quo, he tries to live in the no-man's-land between godliness and worldliness. Curiously, the word from which we derive our word *apathy* (Greek *apeitheia,* which means "indifference" or "without feeling") is usually translated "disobedience" in the New Testament (Romans 11:30-32; Ephesians 2:2; 5:6; Hebrews 4:6-11).[9] Apathy leads to disobedience. If we don't care, we won't act. But Jesus finds such lukewarmness nauseating (Revelation 3:16). "No one can serve two masters," the Lord said (Matthew 6:24).

## How to Help a Doubter

Let's be honest. There's no foolproof way to insulate our faith against life's hard questions; and no matter how many answers we provide, we can't guarantee how our doubting friends will respond.

When the apostle Paul preached about "the unknown God" (Acts 17:23) and mentioned the resurrection of Christ to a skeptical crowd in Athens, his message resulted in three responses (vv. 32-34):

1. "Some of them sneered."
2. "Others said, 'We want to hear you again on this subject.'"
3. "A few . . . believed."

When we speak the truth about the Lord, those are common reactions. Some will sneer, some will believe, and others at least will leave the door open for further conversation.

I have engaged in conversations about the Lord with friends and then watched in awe as they accepted the Lord, grew in their faith, and remained steadfast in their commitment through the years. I also know the heartache of seeing friends and loved ones reject the gospel and turn away from the truth. I have seen people I considered strong believers drift into skepticism and unbelief, and I have seen hard-hearted rebels turn toward God in humility and repentance.

Remember the parable of the sower? It teaches that when the seed of God's Word is planted, it falls on different kinds of soil, which represent the hearts of the hearers. Jesus said that some who hear God's Word are "hard soil"—the Word never penetrates. Some are "shallow soil"—the Word sprouts but doesn't take root. Some are "thorny soil"—too tangled up in worldly things to bear any fruit. But others are "good soil"—they receive the Word and bear large amounts of fruit for God (Mark 4:15-20).

We shouldn't be surprised when our efforts to share the gospel bring mixed results. We can't control the outcome of the harvest, but we can be faithful in planting the seed.

And what about our friends who *do* believe in Christ, but their questions never seem to let up? The Bible says, "Be merciful to those who doubt" (Jude 22), so we must make every effort to help those who are asking honest questions. There's a big difference between sinful doubt and faith under stress. When you're dealing with a believer, here are three suggestions for handling "faith stress":

1. Be willing to intervene. Some of our friends find relief simply by being able to talk about their questions without receiving instant condemnation and rejection.
2. Be careful about your own attitude. It's wise to approach any kind of spiritual intervention with the humble caution the apostle Paul prescribed in Galatians 6:1, 2: "If someone is caught in a sin, you who are spiritual should restore him gently. But watch yourself, or you also may be tempted."
3. Provide assistance in identifying the kind and cause of the doubt. This can help believers who struggle with false guilt because of their questions.

Sometimes, as Os Guinness notes, "instead of speaking clearly, faith is stammering with fright or choked with pain. But such doubt is still *faith* stammering, *faith* stumbling, *faith* being strangled. Whatever pressure it is under and however strange it sounds, it's not unbelief—at least, not until it gives up and turns back or goes over to the other side."[10] It's important to distinguish between willful disbelief and faith undergoing the painful process of growth.

## Potential Remedies

Let's revisit the different kinds of doubt described in this chapter and offer a potential remedy for each one.

*Slow of heart.* If your doubtful friend is slow to believe because he simply lacks information, lend him a book (perhaps this one!), bring him with you to a small group, meet with him for coffee and help him find the information he needs. Teach him "with great patience and careful instruction" (2 Timothy 4:2). As someone has said, "Feed your faith, and your doubts will starve to death."

*Troubled heart.* If the problem is perplexity, pray that God will give your friend wisdom. Our heavenly Father delights to answer our requests for wisdom with a resounding yes (see James 1:5).

*Faint of heart.* If the problem is weariness, help your friend obtain the kind of rest that will nurture his soul—a spiritual retreat, a vacation, or even just a good night's sleep. Before sending Elijah back into the fray, God made sure he was fed and refreshed by hours of sleep (1 Kings 19:5-9).

*Fearful heart.* If the problem is inadequacy, nothing works better than the kind of healthy encouragement a person can receive in the fellowship of believers (see 1 Thessalonians

> Believe your beliefs and doubt your doubts.[11]
>
> F. F. Bosworth

5:14). Invite your friend to attend church or a small group with you. If he's already a Christian, help him discover his spiritual gifts so he can find a place of satisfying ministry in the body of Christ.

*Wounded heart.* People who have been disillusioned need us to patiently regain their trust. Over time, our consistent example and steady love will earn their respect as they observe our efforts to do what is right both to them and to God (2 Corinthians 8:21).

*Stubborn heart.* When stubborn unbelief (a hard heart) causes a friend to reject all evidence for faith, we need to prayerfully engage in spiritual warfare, asking God to break down Satan's strongholds (see 2 Corinthians 10:3-5).

*Rebellious heart.* If the problem is unsubmissiveness, we need to tactfully but firmly confront the moral issues that lie behind our friend's intellectual objections. This requires courage and careful discernment. Jude tells us to "be merciful to those who doubt," but he also says there are others who need to be snatched "from the fire" (Jude 22, 23). James dared to confront some double-minded friends with these bold words: "Come near to God and he will come near to you. Wash your hands, you sinners, and purify your hearts, you double-minded" (James 4:8).

*Divided heart.* Finally, those afflicted by the doubt of complacency need encouragement to commit themselves firmly and wholeheartedly to the Lord. As Joshua put it, "Choose for yourselves this day whom you will serve. . . . As for me and my household, we will serve the LORD" (Joshua 24:15). On Mount Carmel, Elijah challenged the people, "How long will you waver between two opinions? If the LORD is God, follow him; but if Baal is God, follow him" (1 Kings 18:21).

## Betting on God

The French philosopher, mathematician, and physicist Blaise Pascal (1623–1662) stated what has become known as Pascal's Wager. Basically he argued that a rational person should wager that God exists, because if you live as if there is a God, you have everything to gain and nothing to lose. There are a number of flaws in the argument, but Pascal makes a tantalizing point. If eternal life or death hangs in the balance, doesn't it make sense to tip the scales in the direction of faith?[12]

When it comes to high-stakes living, not many equal the story of Paul Janszen.[13] Paul is famous and infamous for his testimony about Pete Rose's gambling on baseball. For a while, Paul was Pete's buddy, bodyguard, and go-to guy for placing bets with bookies. Paul lived fast and free, juicing himself and others with steroids. There's not much Paul hasn't seen or done.

But one day that changed. Through a series of defining moments in his relationship with Pete and with God, Paul's life took a dramatic turn. He was introduced to a God who loves like no other.

Although Paul still had some skepticism, he began to incrementally walk back to God. He came clean with himself, Major League Baseball, and law enforcement. While Pete Rose continued to deny that he bet on baseball, Paul could no longer deny the truth. He fully confessed—and paid a high price—but is now free (both physically and spiritually).

Through friends, Paul eventually found his way to Whitewater Crossing Christian Church in Cincinnati, Ohio, and now is an example of what God can do when someone fully trusts in him. Even though Paul still has some doubts, he is placing his trust in the God who works all things together for good.

Paul now shares his Christian testimony on a regular basis. His minister, David Vaughan, says, "God is still working on Paul, but clearly he is not the man he used to be. The old Paul is gone, and the new Paul has come. God's grace has covered his disgrace, and God has a new plan for his life. His wife and friends can all attest to this, and he is a hall of famer in their eyes!"

The old hymn by Charlotte Elliott says it well: "Just as I am, though tossed about with many a conflict, many a doubt, fightings and fears within, without, O Lamb of God, I come, I come."[14]

Do you have a friend who struggles with doubt? Reach out to him or her in love. Are you a doubter asking honest questions? God wants you to come to him just as you are.

# Honest Questions for Personal Reflection

1. What has been your most troubling doubt about the Christian faith? Have you resolved it satisfactorily? If so, how? If not, why not?

2. Do you find it natural to talk openly with other people about your faith questions? Why or why not?

# Honest Questions for Group Discussion

## Relate

1. Which of the following best illustrates how you usually deal with your questions about faith?

\_\_\_\_ I talk about them openly and seek to resolve them through conversation.

\_\_\_\_ I keep them to myself, for my faith is a private matter to me.

\_\_\_\_ I read books, magazines, or online articles and seek to resolve my questions through my own study and research.

\_\_\_\_ I ask a trusted friend for advice.

\_\_\_\_ Other:

2. When is it a sin to doubt? Or is it ever? Explain your answer.

## Reflect

3. Read Jude 22. Why do you suppose this verse is in the Bible?

4. The story of one of the most famous doubters of all time is recorded in John 20:19-29. Read this Scripture and discuss:

• What and why did Thomas doubt?

• What evidence did Jesus give Thomas to help him over-come his doubts?

• What was Thomas's response?

• How do you feel about Jesus' words in John 20:29?

• What would it take for you to "stop doubting and believe," as Jesus told Thomas?

5. Read James 1:2-8. What does this Scripture say about the attitude a person should have when his faith is tested? What word pictures found in this Scripture illustrate what it's like to struggle with doubt? According to this Scripture, where does true wisdom come from? (See also James 3:13-17.)

6. How can you help someone survive a severe bout with "faith stress"? What kind of attitude should you have when you get involved with this kind of problem? (See Galatians 6:1, 2; James 5:19, 20; Jude 22, 23.)

## Respond

7. What doubts have been holding you back in your service to the Lord? In the spirit of James 5:16 ("Confess your sins to each other and pray for each other so that you may be healed"), share with the group some area of sin or stress that has been hindering your commitment to Christ.

8. Select two volunteers to lead the group in a closing prayer. One person should focus on a prayer of confession, and the other on thanksgiving for God's gracious forgiveness. (See 1 John 1:7-10 for ideas.)

# Resources for Further Study

*Doubting: Growing Through the Uncertainties of Faith* by Alister McGrath (Downers Grove, IL: InterVarsity Press, 2006)

*God in the Dark: The Assurance of Faith Beyond a Shadow of Doubt* by Os Guinness (Wheaton, IL: Crossway Books, 1996)

*The Apologetics of Jesus: A Caring Approach to Dealing with Doubters* by Norman L. Geisler and Patrick Zukeran (Grand Rapids, MI: Baker Books, 2009)

*The Thomas Factor: Using Your Doubts to Draw Closer to God* by Gary R. Habermas (Nashville, TN: Broadman & Holman, 1999)

## Chapter 5

# Why Did God Let This Happen?

**We shall draw from the heart of suffering itself the means of inspiration and survival.** **Winston Churchill**

BRANDON, age twenty-three, was stationed far from his home in Michigan, serving with the U. S. military in Iraq.[1] In an e-mail, he shared his struggles over the death of his sergeant and four other soldiers the week before. He was trying to come to grips with the casualties of war in a world that seemed so full of darkness and pain. He wrote:

You know, when faced with hardship in our lives, most of us turn to questions of why. I can tell you that whether you are in Grand Rapids, Michigan, or in Baghdad, Iraq, these questions are typical of a person faced with hardship and sacrifice. So naturally, you can imagine that after all the other emotions had ripped through my mind, one of my first questions was to ask the Lord, "Why? Why, Lord, would you allow this to happen? Why would you let me experience this? Why would you let this happen to such good people? Why have you thrust me into this situation? Why is our country involved in a place where the people want to kill us?"

A month after writing that e-mail, on January 22, 2007, Brandon was killed in the line of duty.

SUE ANN stood outside the church door late on a Saturday night.[2] Her loud knocking echoed all the way up to the second-floor office, catching the attention of the minister working there. Her eyes filled with tears, Sue Ann looked as if she didn't have a hope in the world—and in fact, she didn't.

The minister invited her in, and she related her story. She was nineteen years old and on her way to commit suicide. Driving past the church building, she noticed a light still on and pulled into the parking lot, hoping to find a reason to go on living.

She said that her father began to sexually abuse her at a young age. He would come home drunk; and after physically abusing her mother, he would turn his attention to her. She noticed that when she approached her dad first and acquiesced to his advances, he would leave her mother alone. She felt ashamed, demeaned, and completely disillusioned, but she had been willing to endure it all for the sake of her mother. The abuse continued for years.

Now her younger sister was coming of age, and their father was starting to do the same thing to her. Sue Ann couldn't endure that. She had given up hope.

BEV grew up in Chicago.[3] Her father, a respected physician, led the department of physical therapy at a local hospital.

"People would come from Europe so Dad could treat them," Bev remembered. "He was a good doctor. He never said no to anybody. Besides working at the hospital, he'd make house calls."

One night Bev's mom and dad decided to go out for dinner with friends. Her dad took her to the house where she was to babysit that evening. Playing with the children, she waved good-bye as her dad drove away in his olive-green Buick Electra.

It was the last time Bev saw her dad alive. He died that night from a massive heart attack. He was forty-one. She was fourteen.

"I've always felt that I was cheated," Bev lamented. "He died before I got to know him. Why was he taken from me?"

She received little assistance with her questions because her mother felt the same way. "Mom had no one to help her, and she asked for no help. It was tough for all of us for a while."

In the aftermath of her dad's death, Bev's friends and relatives tried to offer words of comfort, but there was something hollow about it all. God had rarely been mentioned in Bev's home, except during the holidays when someone would say a mealtime prayer. And when she became a teenager, her parents had told her it was her choice whether she'd go to church or not. She chose not to go.

As time went on, Bev often felt something was missing, but all she felt toward God was anger. She wondered, *Why did you take my dad away from me, God—right when I needed him most?*

Bev recalled an incident that took place after her father died: "I was home alone when one of my boyfriend's buddies rang the doorbell at 6:00 in the morning. He said he was too drunk to drive home, and he wanted to come in and lie down on the living room couch for a while. Something in my heart said, *Don't let him in,* but I said OK, let him in, and then went back to bed. A few minutes later, he came into my bedroom and raped me. I didn't report it. It was the first of four times I was sexually attacked—in part, I think, because I kept putting myself into dangerous situations. I thought that sex—even sex with someone I didn't know or care about—was at least a way to feel loved."

Bev graduated from high school and, still angry with a God she didn't trust, began using drugs (especially marijuana) to fill the void. "Pot would relax me and make me feel like a part of the crowd," she said. "I took uppers and speed; but then I had to drink to come down, so I was drunk a lot of the time."

Married at age twenty-nine, Bev and her husband frequently used drugs together; but after having two babies, Bev was determined to quit. "I knew that if I was going to keep my life together and raise two kids, I couldn't do it while I was on drugs," she said. With help from a rehab program and an employees assistance program at work, Bev managed to stay drug-free for years.

But she continued to wonder, *If there is a God, why does he let so many bad things happen in a person's life?*

Do the questions asked by Brandon, Sue Ann, and Bev resonate with you? Who hasn't wondered about life's unfairness? Who hasn't struggled to overcome hurts from the past? Who hasn't wondered why God doesn't always intervene when bad things happen?

Unless you're an experienced counselor, you might feel stymied when a friend comes to you with honest questions like these. While you and I may not be able to offer the kind of in-depth counseling that can untangle the knots from a person's past, there are some ways ordinary believers can make a big difference if we're willing to come alongside our friends and respectfully, gently share with them the reason for our hope (1 Peter 3:15).

## Counterproductive Approaches

First, let me point out four counterproductive approaches—some unhelpful things we should *not* do or say when someone comes asking, "Why did God let this happen?"

*1. Avoiding.* When a person expresses anger toward God, we may not want to get involved. Why befriend someone like Sue Ann or Bev who carries so much baggage from the past? Who needs another high-maintenance relationship?

Jesus didn't take that approach. He didn't stay in an ivory tower in Heaven so he could avoid tough situations and difficult people. He came to earth as Immanuel, "God with us" (Matthew 1:23). He touched people who had leprosy. He dined with well-known sinners. He mingled with rough-cut carpenters, fishermen, and soldiers. He pursued a life-changing conversation with a Samaritan woman whose past included five husbands and whose present included a live-in companion.

Avoid people who are hurting? Not if we're going to follow in Jesus' footsteps.

*2. Minimizing.* Some Christians downplay life's unfairness. They deal with heartaches stoically, toughing it out with a stiff upper lip. Others adopt an oversimplified approach and offer theological platitudes like, "Don't worry, everything will work out for good" or "Just pray and you'll feel better." Still others attempt to minimize suffering through an indifferent attitude that says, "Yeah, well, life is tough all over. I could tell you about some problems of my own!"

> He jests at scars that never felt a wound.[4]
>
> William Shakespeare

The problem of life's unfairness is as old as the first tear and as recent as the latest news. More than four hundred years before Christ, people were asking, "Where is the God of justice?" (Malachi 2:17).

We search for a reasonable explanation of how God can be just even though he allows evil to exist in the world. Philosophers have a name for this search: *theodicy*—"defense of God's goodness and omnipotence in view of the existence of evil."[5]

- Health fails.
- A plane crashes.
- A factory lays off workers.
- A young mom comes home to find her husband gone.
- A baby dies.
- A tornado devastates a town.
- With one wrong turn of the steering wheel, a teenager leaves behind dozens of grieving relatives and friends.
- A husband and wife with a strong marriage want to be parents but discover they are infertile, while a fifteen-year-old girl gets pregnant after one sexual encounter with a boy she'll never see again.
- A white-collar criminal bilks millions of dollars from unsuspecting victims, then emerges from court smiling, as he prepares to serve a light sentence that amounts to little more than a slap on the wrist.

People want to know why. They ask hard questions every day in hospital rooms and funeral homes, at accident scenes and gravesites, in hushed conversations in doctors' offices and in the silent doubts of their own minds. If God is powerful and loving, why doesn't he intervene? We shouldn't minimize such serious questions.

*3. Blaming.* Another counterproductive technique is blaming.

"No wonder you've had problems," a hard-liner might say to Bev. "What do you expect? You brought it on yourself by ignoring God, using drugs, and violating God's standards of sexual purity."

There is a kernel of truth in this point of view. The Bible teaches, "Do not be deceived: God cannot be mocked. A man reaps what he sows" (Galatians 6:7). Much human suffering results from our own foolish choices, and we have no one to blame but ourselves. As Proverbs 19:3 points out, "A man's own folly ruins his life, yet his heart rages against the LORD." We shouldn't blame God for problems of our own making. But even if the trouble *is* the person's own fault, the right time to discuss it is not when the person is at the height of pain.

Not all suffering can be explained as the direct consequence of our own personal sin. Jesus never sinned, but he suffered intensely. Job was a "blameless and upright" man who "feared God and shunned evil" (Job 1:1), yet he endured one hardship after another.

When Jesus came upon a man who had been blind since birth, the disciples tried to find someone to blame. They asked, "Rabbi, who sinned, this man or his parents, that he was born blind?" And Jesus responded, "Neither this man nor his parents sinned, . . . but this happened so that the work of God might be displayed in his life" (John 9:2, 3).

Some of life's sorrows result from our own sinful misuse of God-given freedom; some from the sins of others; some from the direct attacks of Satan; some from natural laws God has ordained to operate in our world (and in a broken world, natural laws sometimes result in unnatural harm).

All human suffering is traceable to Adam and Eve's disobedience in the Garden of Eden that resulted in death for humanity and a world "subjected to frustration," in "bondage to decay," and "groaning as in the pains of childbirth" (Genesis 3; Romans 8:18-22). Car accidents, heart attacks, and emotional anguish should come as no surprise in this sin-tarnished world that the Bible describes with unvarnished realism. That's why Jesus stated so honestly, "In this world you will have trouble" (John 16:33). It's why 1 Peter 4:12 bluntly warns, "Dear friends, do not be surprised at the painful trial you are suffering, as though something strange were happening to you." As someone has said, to be surprised by suffering is to be surprised that something Jesus predicted has actually come true!

Bad things happen routinely enough that you can't always pin the blame on any specific sin a person has committed.[6]

4. *Pitying.* Pitying doesn't help much either. When Jesus encountered a grieving widow on her way to bury her only son, "his heart went out to her" (Luke 7:13). Then he spoke to her and raised her son from the dead. At the tomb of Jesus' friend Lazarus, "Jesus wept" (John 11:35). And he not only cared enough to weep; he was willing to stick around and intervene, bringing hope to his grieving friends. Jesus didn't stop with mere thoughts of pity. He *acted* on that pity!

God calls us to do more than feel sorry; he calls us to act, to "be kind and compassionate to one another" (Ephesians 4:32).

## Constructive Approaches

Let's be honest. Pain and grief are unwelcome facts of life. But in Christ we do not "grieve like the rest of men, who have no hope" (1 Thessalonians 4:13). Our hope in Christ makes all the difference when we confront life's hurts and injustices.

So what *are* some better ways to handle the honest questions of those who feel angry or disappointed with God?

A beginning point is to acknowledge that anger itself can be an expression of faith. You can't be angry with someone who doesn't exist! To feel angry with God is to admit, at least, that he is there. Analyzing the suffering of Job, Glandion Carney and William Long point out that "Job was angry principally because he *did* believe, deep down, that God is a just and good God and that therefore what happened to him was unjust and should be rectified."[7]

When a friend directs angry questions toward God, his spiritual journey doesn't need to come to an end. The journey may be just beginning. Here are four needs to keep in mind as you seek to assist your friend.

## 1. Practical help

*Love* is a fine-sounding noun, but in the rough and tumble of real life, it needs to be a verb. Our hurting friends ask, "Why did God let this happen?" But they may not need us to *speak up* as much as simply to *show up* and help with practical matters like preparing a meal, cleaning the house or doing the laundry, paying a bill, watching the kids, helping with 24/7 caregiving, assisting with funeral arrangements, making phone calls, or shopping for groceries.

When someone asks why God "let this happen," our first response shouldn't be to act like a philosopher but to act like a friend.

> Jesus Christ laid down his life for us. And we ought to lay down our lives for our brothers. If anyone has material possessions and sees his brother in need but has no pity on him, how can the love of God be in him? Dear children, let us not love with words or tongue but with actions and in truth.
>
> the apostle John
>
> (1 John 3:16-18)

## 2. Emotional release

I used to consider it odd when people cried because their dogs died. Then I got a dog of my own. After twelve years of bonding with my cocker spaniel, I was amazed how sad I felt on the day she died—but any true dog lover won't find my sorrow the least bit surprising.

Emotions run deep. They influence our decisions and sometimes cloud our judgment. A friend of mine advises, "Don't try to answer an intellectual question with an emotional answer, and don't try to answer an emotional question with an intellectual answer." A wounded sufferer doesn't need a scolding or an argument as much as she needs someone to empathize with her pain. We shouldn't short-circuit grief. The grief process is part of our God-given emotional equipment for dealing with a loss-prone world.

Job endured the destruction of his property, the deaths of his children, and painful sores all over his body. Hearing what had happened, his friends came to comfort him. The Bible says, "When they saw him from a distance, they could hardly recognize him; they began to weep aloud, and they tore their robes and sprinkled dust on their heads. Then they sat on the ground with him for seven days and seven nights. No one said a word to him, because they saw how great his suffering was" (Job 2:12, 13). They sat with him silently for a whole week! In fact, when you read their comments recorded later in the book of Job and the theories they espoused to explain Job's suffering, you wonder if they may have been the most help to him when they kept their mouths shut and simply sat quietly at his side.

When someone is hurting, true friends don't lead with a lecture; they listen, and listen well. True friends "rejoice with those who rejoice" and "mourn with those who mourn" (Romans 12:15).

## 3. Theological balance

Of all the questions people ask, queries about suffering are some of the hardest. I have found it helpful to point questioning friends toward two concepts: "The Elusive Why" and "The Ever-Present Who."

### The Elusive Why

One terrible day my wife, children, and I came home from church to find our house surrounded by firefighters and half our possessions destroyed by fire. In the aftermath I asked the Lord lots of questions. Why did the fire happen? From one perspective, it was easy to answer: a fan overheated in my son's bedroom. From a larger perspective, I will never know why. Was there some cosmic reason in the mind of God? Did my family need to go through that experience to teach us some spiritual lessons? Perhaps. All I know is, in the midst of the mess, we experienced the love of God not merely as a noun but as a verb—as Christian friends brought an ice cream pie to lift our spirits, gave us toys to replace the ones our children lost in the fire, handed us cash to buy new clothes, and invited us to dinner while the house was being rebuilt.

The "why" question is hard to answer. Whether or not you believe in God, life will always have its mysteries, especially the mysteries of suffering. Just as a child doesn't understand everything his parents say and do, God's ways often appear bewildering to us. Deuteronomy 29:29 says, "The secret things belong to the LORD our God, but the things revealed belong to us and to our children forever, that we may follow all the words of this law." There are mysteries ("secret things") we can't understand about God or about life. But God has revealed much that we *can* understand and obey—enough to keep us busy for a lifetime.

Most of us don't pay enough attention to God and others when things are going well. C. S. Lewis wrote that pain is God's "megaphone to rouse a deaf world."[8] Life's hurts compel us to think about the devastating consequences of sin, our need for God's grace, and the brevity of life. "Why, you do not even know what will happen tomorrow. What is your life? You are a mist that appears for a little while and then vanishes" (James 4:14).

The apostle Paul experienced The Elusive Why while he endured what he termed "a thorn in my flesh" (2 Corinthians 12:7). The Bible doesn't tell us the exact identity of Paul's "thorn," which is good because all of us can relate to it no matter what struggles we may face. Most of us, I suspect, have a thorn in the flesh, and it's not always clear why. Author R. T. Kendall says, "For some it is a handicap or disability. It could be unhappy employment—or even lack of employment. It may be a job that you are locked into. It could be an enemy. It could be loneliness. It could be coping with unhappy living conditions. It could be a sexual misgiving. It could be an unhappy marriage. It could be chronic illness. It could be a personality problem. It could have to do with money matters. It could be an unwanted calling. The list is endless."[9]

When the Father in Heaven allows a thorn to puncture our pride, he does it so we will learn to rely on his grace instead of our own strength. Three times I pleaded with the Lord to take [the thorn] away from me," wrote the apostle Paul. "But he said to me, 'My grace is sufficient for you, for my power is made perfect in weakness'" (2 Corinthians 12:8, 9). The troublesome "why" may always elude us. But God is . . .

## THE EVER-PRESENT WHO

While a friend of mine was in law school, his wife miscarried their second child, and someone asked whether going through the miscarriage shook their faith.

"No," my friend explained. "My faith is founded on a sufferer. Therefore, I fully anticipate going through difficult times when God feels distant."

The heart of the gospel—the ultimate answer to the problem of evil—rests in the divine-human sufferer, Jesus Christ. Author Philip Yancey has asked, "Where is God when it hurts?" The answer is, "Right here with us." The Lord is The Ever-Present Who—"an ever-present help in trouble" (Psalm 46:1).

To be honest, it doesn't always feel that way. One chapter before the psalmist said "The LORD is my shepherd" (Psalm 23:1), he complained, "My God, my God, why have you forsaken me?" (22:1). We can't always explain why bad things happen to good people. But we can be sure that God isn't aloof, detached, and unaffected by our sorrows. Jesus Christ shows that he is a vulnerable (woundable) God who takes our pain upon himself. Hard questions about suffering cannot find resolution in philosophical arguments alone, but in the one who came to earth and confronted the problem of evil in person. If we complain that "bad things happen to good people," we need to remember that the worst thing happened to the best of people, the Son of God himself.

Remember Sue Ann, the woman who stopped at a church as she was contemplating suicide? The minister told her that the Father's love for her knew no bounds. They talked about Jesus and how his death and resurrection can change a life of shame to a life of meaning and significance. They talked about the Holy Spirit and how he can fill a life with hope. After a couple of hours, she left the minister's office promising to be at church the next morning, but she didn't show. The minister was concerned she had done herself harm. But three weeks later she came to church on a Sunday morning and came forward at the end of the service to give her life to Christ and be baptized into the family of God.

As Sue Ann's faith grew, eventually she led her sister, brother, and mother to Jesus. She even managed to forgive her father, who stopped abusing his family and also started attending church. Does every story of suffering have such a happy ending? No, but real change is possible with Christ, The Ever-Present Who.

And here's an amazing truth: The Ever-Present Who wants to work through Ordinary You!

## 4. Connection with fellow sufferers

Think of it this way: When Jesus died on the cross, his back was torn by the beating he'd endured. His head bled from the crown of thorns. His mouth was parched from thirst. His side was ripped open by a spear. His hands and feet were pierced by the nails. All the muscles, bones, and nerves in his body were affected. Inwardly, his emotions endured wrenching pain as he bore our sins. Jesus' entire body suffered on the cross.

Likewise, when one part of Jesus' *spiritual* body (the church) suffers "every part suffers with it" (1 Corinthians 12:26). Suffering seems more intense when we face it alone, but it grows more bearable when we are surrounded by a community of caring believers. People who grieve painful losses often find comfort and growth when they're able to open up and talk about their experiences with others.

Several years ago Tom Lawson suffered through the sudden death of his first wife. Reflecting on what brought him comfort, Lawson wrote:

God comforts us in our suffering (through the presence of

the Holy Spirit and through the love of other people) so that we can provide that same comfort to others (2 Corinthians 1:3-7). The parents who lost an infant find themselves drawn to the young couple in the church whose baby just died. The man who was laid off last year finds himself having coffee with a member of his Sunday school class whose business went under.

"Why?" is less awkward when you remember your own moments of grief, confusion, and pain. You just reach up and brush aside your own tears, hold out your arms, and offer your friends a shoulder to cry on. And more often than not you find your own tears wetting their shoulders, even as their tears touch yours.

It is that image, even more than faces bright with smiles, that demonstrates the power and presence of the Holy Spirit in the life of the church. People with hurts of their own reach out to others who are hurting, and both find the presence of God. . . . Here questions are laid aside, human pride dissolves, and all the masks fall away. Here, if we would only open our hearts to see, is the very presence of the Spirit of God in our midst.[10]

There's something about connecting with other people—especially others who have gone through their own seasons of suffering—that helps us experience God's presence and power. Remember Bev, the woman whose dad died suddenly when she was fourteen? She was angry and confused about God, so when a neighbor invited Bev to a church barbecue, she resisted at first, but finally decided to attend. She was surprised at the friendly reception she received.

"Many people talked with me," she said. "They weren't walking around singing hymns and doing whatever I thought religious people did. They were laughing, eating hamburgers, playing volleyball. And there were so many children—happy, laughing children."

When her friend said, "Maybe you'd like to meet Mark," Bev was surprised again.

"I didn't know you could call your priest—your minister, or whatever—by his first name! That was unheard of where I came from! It sounded disrespectful. But I did meet with him, and that's where it all started." Her minister introduced her to Christ, but before Jesus became her Lord, a caring neighbor became her friend.

## Beyond Asking Why

"Why does God allow bad things to happen?" When pondering that question, no book offers more profound insights than the Old Testament book of Job. Bob Russell, retired senior minister of Southeast Christian Church in Louisville, Kentucky, identified five principles from studying that book:

1. Human suffering is not easy to explain. Don't always try.
2. Being good does not exempt us from calamity. Don't expect it to.
3. God is not the author of most suffering, so don't blame him.
4. Genuine faith does not require immediate answers, but anticipates ultimate justice. Don't doubt.
5. God's blessings are promised to those who persevere. Don't quit.[11]

Imagine finding a silver dollar on the sidewalk. The coin is tarnished and dented. You can speculate about why it's in such bad shape. You may never know exactly what happened to it. But one thing's for sure: that tarnished coin still has value! You would be foolish to throw it away instead of spending it wisely.

Your life may be tarnished and dented. You may not know why. But your life still has incredible value. Somewhere I read that God doesn't always explain everything we would like to know about the "genesis of our suffering, but he always reassures us that there's an "exodus"—a way out. You need to spend your life wisely, not throw it away.

Remember Brandon, the soldier mentioned at the beginning of this chapter? While in Iraq he worked with a tiny church where the Iraqi Christians were undergoing severe persecution. It was dangerous to be seen worshipping together, yet the Iraqi Christians never missed a Sunday service. Brandon worshipped with them, encouraging them to carry on. He was especially drawn to the children who had witnessed so much suffering and death. Brandon was proud to be a soldier for the United States, but he was even prouder to be a soldier for the Lord.

Brandon had questioned the Lord and wondered why he was facing so much suffering there in Iraq. But here's the rest of what Brandon wrote in that e-mail, written just a few days before his death:

> God led me back to his Word, back to Paul's second letter to Timothy. In the second chapter Paul states, "You then, my son, be strong in the grace that is in Christ Jesus. And the things you have heard me say in the presence of many witnesses entrust to reliable men who will also be qualified to teach others. Endure hardship with us like a good soldier of Christ Jesus. . . . Reflect on what I am saying, for the Lord will give you insight into all this" (2 Timothy 2:1-3, 7).
>
> Paul's writings really opened my eyes about the enduring part of hardship. They also spoke loudly to me about my question, "Why?" Why doesn't matter! Asking why is not the understanding Paul is talking about. It is the understanding of our relationship with God that we should strive for! Hardship and sacrifice—this is all part of the work that we must put into forming a great relationship with God. This is how we can live to please the One who enrolled us as soldiers in the first place. I no longer concern myself with why. Why, to me, wastes time. I cannot afford to waste time when the Word of God tells me, "And the things you have heard me say in the presence of

many witnesses entrust to reliable men who will also be qualified to teach others." That is a pretty clear message concerning my duty as a soldier! Thanks be to my God for his Word in which I am able to find peace and understanding.

The Lord never dismisses a wounded questioner with a condescending pat on the head, and neither should we. Human nature says "I feel bad for you" while walking away, but God's love says "I understand what you're going through" and sticks around to help.

So how should we respond when a friend asks, "Why did God let this happen?" Offer hands to help. Provide a shoulder to cry on. Acknowledge The Elusive Why. Point to The Ever-Present Who. Embrace your friend in the supportive fellowship of the church.

And most of all, remember what Jesus teaches in John 16:33. Be realistic about suffering. (He said, "In this world you will have trouble.") But don't consider yourself a permanent victim of it. (He also said, "Take heart! I have overcome the world.")

Suffering doesn't have the last word. Jesus does.

# Honest Questions for Personal Reflection

1. When you have experienced suffering, what was the main question you asked?

\_\_\_ "Why did God let this happen?"
\_\_\_ "How did I get myself into this mess?"
\_\_\_ "How (or What) can I get out of this experience?"
\_\_\_ Other:

2. Read Romans 8:28. How have you discovered the truth of this verse in the midst of your own hardships?

# Honest Questions for Group Discussion

## Relate

1. Tell the group about one of the following:

A. the first time you ever broke a bone
B. the first time you visited a hospital emergency room
C. the worst pain you ever experienced
D. your most interesting scar

2. Which kind of pain seems worst to you—physical suffering, emotional suffering, or spiritual suffering? Explain.

## Reflect

3. The Bible is quite honest about life's unfairness and pain. Read and briefly discuss these verses:

- Job 5:7

- Ecclesiastes 9:11, 12

- Habakkuk 1:2, 3

4. "Anger itself can be an expression of faith. You can't be angry with someone who doesn't exist! To feel angry with God is to admit, at least, that he is there" (p. 93). Do you agree or disagree with that statement? Explain.

5. The classic version of the problem of evil asks us to reconcile the following three statements: (1) God is good, (2) God is all-powerful, yet (3) evil exists. In other words, if God is good, wouldn't he destroy evil? And if he's all-powerful, *couldn't* he destroy evil? Yet evil exists, and bad things happen on a daily basis. Christians believe that Jesus, God's Son, is the key to resolving the problem of evil. On the cross, he took our sins upon himself and suffered the penalty we deserve (1 Peter 2:24). This demonstrates God's goodness. When Jesus rose from the dead on the third day, he gave us hope and proved that death doesn't have the last word (1 Corinthians 15:3-8, 55-58). This demonstrates God's power. And by Jesus' willingness to come to earth in person and suffer, he shows that God is not an absentee deity who's unconcerned and aloof while we suffer (Romans 5:1-11). God takes the problem of evil so seriously that he came to earth and threw himself personally into the midst of it, to accomplish his plan of salvation. "The reason the Son of God appeared was to destroy the devil's work" (1 John 3:8). "This is the victory that has overcome the world, even our faith" (1 John 5:4).

What parts of that explanation might you use in discussions with your friends? What *else* might you say to explain (in biblical terms) why a loving God allows suffering to exist?

## Respond

6. Read 1 Peter 4:12-19. List at least four facts this Scripture teaches about suffering and how we should respond to it. Discuss how it is possible to live out those responses.

7. First Peter 5:7 says, "Cast all your anxiety on him because he cares for you." Spend some time in prayer, focusing on the pressures and problems group members are facing today.

# Resources for Further Study

*Evil and the Justice of God* by N. T. Wright (Downers Grove, IL: InterVarsity Press, 2006)

*Second Guessing God: Hanging on When You Can't See His Plan* by Brian Jones (Cincinnati, OH: Standard Publishing, 2006)

*Trusting God Again: Regaining Hope After Disappointment or Loss* by Glandion Carney and William Long (Downers Grove, IL: InterVarsity Press, 1995)

*Where Is God When It Hurts?* (1990) and *Disappointment with God* (1988) by Philip Yancey (Grand Rapids, MI: Zondervan)

*Why a Suffering World Makes Sense* by Chris Tiegreen (Grand Rapids, MI: Baker Books, 2006)

## Chapter 6

# What About My Family's Religious Traditions?

**It ain't so much the things we don't know that get us in trouble. It's the things we know that ain't so.**

Artemus Ward

The port city of Niigata is located on the west coast of Japan, across the Sea of Japan from Russia and China. It was my first visit to Japan, so as my plane made its final approach, I gazed out the window with fascination at the bright green rice paddies laid out in symmetrical designs in the valleys below.

Yoshi (pronounced *YO-shee*) and his daughter Emiko (*EM-ee-ko*, one of my former students) greeted me at the airport with an Asian-style bow and an American-style handshake.[1] I savored the pleasant realization that friendship can transcend cultural barriers even when I'm half a world from home.

## Getting Acquainted

Yoshi had worked at Niigata city hall for more than forty years before retiring to serve as director of a day-care service center for the elderly, people with disabilities, and children. Emiko works as an English instructor. She and her mother are Christians; her father and her two brothers are not.

I knew some things about the country of Japan already, of course, but I enjoyed hearing a native of Japan tell this *gaijin* (foreigner) about local customs.

"Since our country is surrounded by sea," Yoshi explained, "we are able to eat fresh fish all the time. We eat some of it raw—that's sushi. And rice is our daily food."

In Japan I rarely saw a church building or a cross. (It was quite a contrast to South Korea, where I was amazed by the number of growing churches filled with eager Christians praying and worshipping God.)

"Our family religion is traditional," Yoshi said. "Our culture has been influenced by other countries like China and India through many years. There are Buddhist temples and castles here that were built hundreds of years ago."

Making it more personal, Yoshi said, "There are two different kinds of altars that might be in a Japanese home. One is a Buddhist altar, which comforts our ancestors' spirits. Also there is a Shinto altar, which is believed to offer protection of our home. Although," he quickly added, "I don't have personal faith in any gods."

"I hope you understand what he is saying," Emiko interjected. "His point of view about religion is rather complex, yet it seems many people in Japan feel the same way. Many refer to themselves as Buddhists, but they don't necessarily have faith in it. Religious rituals are performed on ceremonial occasions, but often are not a matter of individual faith. For example, it's common for people to ask a Buddhist monk to perform a funeral, whether they have faith in Buddha or not."

Emiko had spent enough time in the United States to offer another observation: "I think Japanese Buddhists are like some Americans who go to church twice a year for Easter and Christmas. Whether they actually believe in Jesus' resurrection or not, it's a common practice."

## At Least It Feels Familiar

Yoshi continued to explain his religion: "I was raised in a culture surrounded by Buddhist temples and Shinto shrines. They are so natural to me. Even though I don't have strong feelings toward them, they are still familiar to me. Many Japanese go to those places to receive their blessings of good luck on occasions like New Year's Day, when they get married, when they have new babies, or even when they get new cars. Those places don't ask us for strong commitment. They don't train people to learn more about Buddhism or Shintoism, unless someone really wants to know."

He paused. "Basically everyone is welcomed. I think that is how they make money," he noted matter-of-factly. "They charge money for prayers, and people give money offerings for luck."

Then Yoshi switched to the topic of Christianity. "However, the Christian church is different," he said. "I feel uncomfortable there because the difference between Christians and non-Christians seems big. And the idea of Hell is unacceptable to me. If I don't follow the Christian God, why must I go to Hell? I don't know about Christian theology, and I don't know the Bible," he admitted. "But this is what I am feeling toward Christians."

## Traditions Are Good, Right?

Remember the classic musical *Fiddler on the Roof*? It begins with the Jewish father, Tevye, singing enthusiastically about the value of tradition. While Tevye's Jewish culture is worlds apart from Yoshi's Japanese culture, at the root of both men's experience is a common respect for tradition. And they both have a point.

While most Americans don't have Buddhist or Shinto altars in their homes, they understand how it feels to be comfortable with cultural traditions. After all, Americans have plenty of their own—from fireworks on the Fourth of July to parades on New Year's Day, from chocolate Valentine's Day hearts to flowers for Mom on Mother's Day.

My family enjoys holiday customs like going to Grandpa and Grandma's farm for Thanksgiving and putting the same old ornaments on the Christmas tree every year. Even though we usually don't give much thought to the way certain customs originated, we follow them anyway. We celebrate birthdays by blowing out candles on a cake and singing an off-key rendition of "Happy Birthday to You." At weddings, the bride and groom place rings on their left hands, and the bride tosses her bouquet over her shoulder.

Why? Who knows?

Churches have traditions too. Before preaching in South Korea, I was advised to remove my shoes. It was a bit uncomfortable standing behind the pulpit on a small cushion in my sock feet, but I was humbled by this simple reminder that proclaiming the Word of God constituted standing on holy ground.

Many things our American culture associates with Christian faith are matters of tradition, not biblical requirements: from steeples to pulpits, from the style of music we sing to the way we celebrate Christ's birth on December 25.

Christian traditions can be valuable. They link us with past generations of believers—their wisdom, their celebrations, their love for God. Like the roots of a healthy plant, tra-

> Tradition is a guide and not a jailer.[2]
>
> W. Somerset Maugham

ditions give us stability in changing times. They remind us that we are part of a great heritage of faith. They nurture our sense of history and connect us with the church through the ages.

But there's another side to the story. Before responding to Yoshi's concerns, let's examine our own cultural biases and take a look at what the Bible says about problems with religious tradition.

## The Problem with Tradition

Jesus lived in a Jewish culture saturated with tradition. His words recorded in Mark 7 help us identify five problems with religious tradition.

### 1. Tradition can cause us to emphasize the unimportant

Some of the Pharisees and teachers of the law saw that Jesus' disciples were eating their food with "unclean" hands. The issue wasn't a matter of hygiene; it was a matter of ceremony. Before every meal, the Pharisees went through an elaborate hand-washing ritual, pouring water over their hands in certain prescribed ways to symbolically rinse away any impurities from sin.

As Mark puts it, "The Pharisees and all the Jews do not eat unless they give their hands a ceremonial washing, holding to the tradition of the elders. When they come from the marketplace they do not eat unless they wash. And they observe many other traditions, such as the washing of cups, pitchers and kettles" (Mark 7:3, 4). When Jesus' disciples ignored these ceremonial washings, their critics considered it more than bad manners; they considered it sin.

Now, God's law did prescribe certain washings to be performed by the priests (Exodus 40:30-32, for example). But the Pharisees had added an encyclopedic pile of regulations to what the Scripture required, and they pressured others to follow their rules—which in many cases were more detailed and difficult to keep than the actual laws of God. In fact, some of the Jews adhered so stubbornly to their hand-washing tradition that one Pharisee, imprisoned by the Romans, nearly died of thirst because when his captors gave him water to drink, he used it for ceremonial washing instead of drinking it![3]

Elsewhere Jesus warned that strict adherence to human tradition can result in overemphasizing minor matters and overlooking the major ones. "Woe to you, teachers of the law and Pharisees, you hypocrites!" His eyes must have flashed indignantly as he spoke. "You give a tenth of your spices . . . but you have neglected the more important matters of the law—justice, mercy and faithfulness. You should have practiced the latter, without neglecting the former. You blind guides! You strain out a gnat but swallow a camel" (Matthew 23:23, 24).

Religious tradition can deceive us into emphasizing things that really aren't important in the eyes of God. We can end up assuming that our relationship with God is mainly about food, clothing, religious objects we wear as jewelry or use to decorate our homes, or even a certain kind of music. But "the kingdom of God is not a matter of eating and drinking, but of righteousness, peace and joy in the Holy Spirit" (Romans 14:17).

## 2. Tradition can cause us to make inaccurate, self-righteous judgments

Mark informs us that Jesus' disciples were so busy assisting crowds of needy people, they barely had time to eat at all (Mark 6:30, 31)—let alone observe all the Pharisees' hand-washing traditions! But the critical traditionalists didn't see the good the disciples were doing and the stress they were enduring; they only saw what was lacking. Confronting Jesus, they demanded, "Why don't your disciples live according to the tradition of the elders instead of eating their food with 'unclean' hands?" (7:5).

If these critics were upset now, I wonder what they thought when Jesus fed five thousand men, plus women and children? All those people were out in the countryside where there weren't any ceremonial water pots. But they were hungry, and Jesus fed them, even though they had to eat with unwashed hands.

These critics were the same guys, remember, who prayed boastfully on street corners and blew trumpets to announce they were giving their offerings (Matthew 6:1-4). "They have received their reward in full," Jesus wryly pointed out. In other words, if they want the applause of their peers, they'll get it—but nothing more. By contrast, our heavenly Father rewards the humble, the meek, the sincere—like the tax collector who cried out earnestly, "God, have mercy on me, a sinner." As Jesus said, "Everyone who exalts himself will be humbled, and he who humbles himself will be exalted" (Luke 18:13, 14).

Religious rules sound impressive: "Do not handle! Do not taste! Do not touch!" But while "such regulations indeed have an appearance of wisdom, with their self-imposed worship, their false humility and their harsh treatment of the body," the fact is, "they are based on human commands and teachings" and "they lack any value in restraining sensual indulgence" (Colossians 2:20-23).

By the way, prideful attitudes can be found in non-traditionalists just as much as in traditionalists. Since the Bible doesn't tell us what kind of clothes we must wear to worship, it's just as wrong to judge those who dress up as it is to judge those who dress down. I've known Christians who criticize any new idea because "we've never done it that way before," and I've known Christians who irrationally refuse to do anything traditional. (Wouldn't many debates in the church fade away if we surrendered our pride and humbly sought to approach God with sincerity and reverence?)

### 3. Tradition often leads to shallow, heartless worship

Jesus told the traditionalists, "Isaiah was right when he prophesied about you hypocrites; as it is written: 'These people honor me with their lips, but their hearts are far from me. They worship me in vain; their teachings are but rules taught by men'" (Mark 7:6, 7). If our hearts are wrong, it's not enough just to say the right words, sing the right songs, or vainly mouth the words of a memorized prayer.

Most traditions start with good intentions, but they can easily degenerate into meaningless habits that merely take us through the motions. If Jesus were preaching to us, would he point out some contradictions between the words of our lips and the condition of our hearts?

### 4. Tradition distracts us from the genuine commands of God

"You have let go of the commands of God and are holding on to the traditions of men," Jesus insisted (Mark 7:8). He gave as an example what some were doing with the Jewish practice of Corban (a gift devoted to God). Instead of using part of their savings or property to help their parents, some of Jesus' contemporaries were telling their parents, basically, "Sorry, we can't help you, because we've devoted our belongings to God." By neglecting their parents, Jesus told them, "you nullify the word of God by your tradition that you have handed down" (vv. 9-13).

No doubt, someone like Yoshi sincerely wants to honor his parents and other ancestors. But we need to honor our parents in a way that pleases the God who created our families, not in a way that offends him.

## 5. Tradition emphasizes outward ceremonies rather than inward realities

Yoshi's daughter Emiko made a good point. Is there really much difference between certain Japanese Buddhists and those American Christians who go to church only at Easter and Christmas even though they don't actually believe in Jesus' resurrection? Isn't it sad when someone assumes it's enough merely to claim the family's religious tradition without any personal commitment? When someone depends on an infant baptism, a confirmation ceremony, or a name written on a church membership list to make him right with God?

Jesus made it clear that one's relationship with God requires an inward commitment, and that sin is a matter of the heart as well as one's actions. "Listen to me, everyone, and understand this," he said. "Nothing outside a man can make him 'unclean' by going into him. Rather, it is what comes out of a man that makes him 'unclean'" (Mark 7:14, 15).

First Peter 1:18 makes an important point when it says, "You know that it was not with perishable things such as silver or gold that you were redeemed from the empty way of life handed down to you from your forefathers."

Even though our forefathers cherished certain traditions, even though they meant well, and even though we may hold strong emotional ties to our ancestors' points of view, we have to be honest and admit: tradition alone can't satisfy our souls, cure our guilty consciences, or give us hope. To accomplish these goals, we need "the precious blood of Christ, a lamb without blemish or defect" (v. 19).

Traditions can be helpful, but only if we recognize them for what they are, keep them flexible, and submit them to the authority of God and his Word. "See to it that no one takes you captive through hollow and deceptive philosophy, which depends on human tradition and the basic principles of this world rather than on Christ" (Colossians 2:8).

## What Can We Say to Yoshi?

Cross-cultural communication is never easy, even when you're simply ordering dinner in an unfamiliar ethnic restaurant. It's even more difficult when you're trying to communicate about matters of eternal truth. Conveying the gospel to someone like Yoshi won't be easy. (Just ask missionaries who have spent their lives serving the Lord in a challenging place like Japan.) Nevertheless, let me offer the following suggestions.

### Be patient

We must never limit what God can do, but the fact is that most of the time, someone like Yoshi will not be won to Christ quickly. His heart, surrounded by layers of resistance and cultural conditioning, will not easily comprehend and accept the good news of Christ.

With him (as with an increasing number of people in American culture today too), our evangelistic method must involve much more than a one-shot approach. It will probably require a patient, painstaking effort to build trust and communicate God's love over a lengthy period of time.

Jesus' parables of the sower, the growing seed, and the mustard seed (Mark 4:1-20, 26-32) suggest that our job is to sow the seed of the gospel in faith, then prayerfully join hands with others—perhaps over a period of many years—who will water the seed and eventually reap the harvest. Sometimes we sow seed and never see results, but if we're planting the true Word of God in others' hearts, we can be confident it will sprout and grow, even when we don't know how (Mark 4:27; see also John 4:34-38; 1 Corinthians 3:5-9).

### Be curious

Ask questions. Listen carefully. You may want to read up on your friend's religion so you can talk intelligently with him about it. Sometimes a more educated conversation can build bridges for the gospel. At the very least, you'll come to know your friend better by understanding his beliefs and culture. And as you compare his religion to Scripture, your own Christian faith can be affirmed and strengthened.

Here are some of the questions I asked Yoshi:

- "Do you see any difference in your daughter since she became a Christian?" (*Yes, he did.*)
- "Do you ever wish you had some of the hope and joy you see in her?"
- "How do you feel about the way the Buddhist priests make money from people?"
- "Does it ever bother you to go through the motions of religious ceremonies even though you don't believe in their power or the gods they represent?"
- "Deep in your heart, have you ever longed to know God personally?"
- "Have you ever wondered if the Christians really are right?"
- "If you could know for sure that you'd go to Heaven when you die, wouldn't you want that assurance?"

11

## Be clear

While we should always handle ourselves with gentleness and respect, there are points we must make clearly and without compromise—whether we're talking with someone like Yoshi or anyone else.

*Christianity isn't about a place; it's about a person (Jesus Christ).* We don't just call people to fulfill a religious obligation by superstitiously appearing in a church building to carry out a prescribed ritual. We call them to worship the Son of God who comes near to us wherever we are (see Acts 17:27; Hebrews 10:22).

*Christianity isn't about luck; it's about faith.* We aren't trying to manipulate spiritual powers for our own benefit. (That's dangerous! See Deuteronomy 18:10-12 and Isaiah 19:1-4.)

> All religions cannot be true at the same time, because they teach many things completely opposite from one another. They all may be wrong, but certainly they all cannot be right.[4]
>
> Josh McDowell

We want to be loyal to the Father in Heaven who cares for us and has revealed how we can live the abundant life (see 2 Peter 1:3).

*Christianity isn't about what your ancestors believe; it's about what you believe.* It's personal. We should respect our elders and maintain a sense of spiritual history (Leviticus 19:32; Deuteronomy 6:20-25), but ultimately each of us must give an account of ourselves to God (Ezekiel 18:20-32; Romans 2:1-16; 2 Corinthians 5:10).

*Christianity isn't about loyalty to one's ethnic group; it's about God's love for all people.* The Bible isn't just about what Yoshi calls "the Christian God"—a god unique to Western religions or limited to certain cultures. It's about the one true God who created all things and all people, who rules over the entire universe, and who sent his Son to give his life so that "whoever believes in him shall not perish but have eternal life" (John 3:16). Jesus told his followers to make disciples "of all nations," or ethnic groups (Matthew 28:19). Heaven will include a great multitude "from every nation, tribe, people and language" (Revelation 7:9).[5]

*Christianity isn't about money; it's about a relationship with God.* Jesus' followers should see money as a blessing from God to be used sincerely, wisely, and generously with proper stewardship (Matthew 6:1-4; Luke 6:38; 12:32-34; 16:10-15). God is pleased with our generosity, but he cannot be bribed or manipulated. We don't earn Brownie points in Heaven by donating money to religious causes. Christians give willingly out of love for the one who first loved us (2 Corinthians 9:6-15; 1 John 3:16-18; 4:19).

*Christianity isn't about leaving people out; it's about bringing them in.* Yoshi feels uncomfortable because there seems to be a big difference between Christians and non-Christians. Is this because Christians leave him out when he attends their meetings with his daughter? Or is it because the message of the cross is confronting Yoshi's heart with a compelling but uncomfortable truth (see 1 Corinthians 1:18-25)? The road to eternal life is indeed narrow (Matthew 7:13, 14), but it's wide enough that Yoshi can walk on it if he chooses to. Christ's invitation is open to him just as much as to anyone else (see 2 Peter 3:9). If he feels like an outsider, he doesn't have to remain one.

*Christianity isn't about condemning people to Hell; it's about saving them from it.* "For God did not send his Son into the world to condemn the world, but to save the world through him. Whoever believes in him is not condemned, but whoever does not believe stands condemned already because he has not believed in the name of God's one and only Son" (John 3:17, 18).

## Be persistent

Yoshi opened the door to further discussion when he acknowledged, "I don't know about Christian theology, and I don't know the Bible." This presents a natural opportunity for a Christian to say, "Would you like to know more? If so, I'll be glad to continue meeting with you to study and discuss these matters."

Someone did that for another man I met in Japan. A few years before, Makoto had bravely become a Christian, despite strong opposition from his family. When I asked what made the difference for him, he pointed to a missionary and said, "Bill studied with me the evidence for Jesus' resurrection. I decided that if Jesus rose from the dead, I needed to follow him, even if that didn't go along with my country's traditions."

## From Islam to Faith in Christ

Nabeel grew up as a devoted Muslim.[6] His parents, immigrants from Pakistan, trained him in his youth to be a Muslim missionary. He memorized much of the Koran, participated in daily prayers, and was deeply committed to Islamic traditions. As a young man Nabeel was trained to challenge Christians about their beliefs. He was told that the Bible was corrupt and Christians weren't really able to defend their faith.

"Show me one place in your Bible where Jesus claimed to be God," Nabeel would demand, and most Christians didn't know how to respond. The few who tried usually pointed to John 14:9 where Jesus said, "Anyone who has seen me has seen the Father." Then Nabeel would point to verse 28 where Jesus said, "The Father is greater than I"—and argue that Jesus wasn't claiming equality with God but picturing his close unity with God. The Christians would be left stammering, and Nabeel would feel smugly superior.

But then Nabeel entered medical school, where he met a well-informed Christian on the debate team, who pointed to other passages where Jesus' deity is plainly taught. For instance:

- "Before Abraham was born, I am!" (John 8:58).
- "In the beginning was the Word, . . . and the Word was God" (John 1:1).
- When Thomas identified the risen Christ as "my Lord and my God" (John 20:28), Jesus accepted the worship and didn't rebuke Thomas for blasphemy.

Nabeel was shaken by the logic of his friend's arguments. Nabeel was the one left stammering, so he decided to study the New Testament more thoroughly to prove his friend wrong. But the more Nabeel studied, the more he was impressed with the character of Jesus and the reliability of the Bible. He then restudied the history of Mohammed, the prophet he had revered all his life. He discovered that, unlike Jesus, Mohammed's life story was far from righteous and certainly not worthy of emulation.

Nabeel was in turmoil for months. Leaving Islam meant losing everything, including his personal identity. One day he prayed for Allah/God to reveal himself to him in a dream, because Muslims place a high value on visions and dreams. Soon he experienced a vivid dream of a narrow door, an archway so small that one could barely squeeze through. On the other side of the door, he could see dozens of joyous people ready to participate in a banquet feast, but they were waiting to begin, as though waiting on a tardy guest to arrive.

The next day Nabeel churned about that dream until he found Luke 13:24-29: "Make every effort to enter though the narrow door. . . . People will come from east and west and north and south, and will take their places at the feast in the kingdom of God."

Not long afterward, Nabeel made a monumental decision to trust in Jesus as God in the flesh. He gave his life to Christ and was baptized into him in a most significant demonstration of his new life.

But Nabeel's commitment to Jesus has not been without a high price. His parents were devastated by his decision and nearly disowned him. He is regarded as a traitor by fellow Muslims and has received vicious hate mail and even a few death threats. In July 2010, he was arrested at an Arabic festival in Dearborn, Michigan, and imprisoned for a night, accused of disturbing the peace simply because he was engaging Muslim attendees in discussions about Jesus.

Today Nabeel has his medical degree, a passion for apologetics, and an intense desire to take the gospel to Muslims.

## In the Final Analysis

In the final analysis, the truth of God matters more than our religious traditions, whether those traditions are Buddhist, Muslim, Jewish . . . or even Christian. We are saved by Christ, not by culture or customs; by grace, not by religious rules. Those unbelievers who are sincerely following the traditions of their ancestors need to hear about "the precious blood of Christ" that can redeem them "from the empty way of life handed down to [them] from [their] forefathers" (1 Peter 1:18, 19).

Nabeel puts it like this: "My mother had never been approached by an evangelical Christian in 35 years. I can't allow that to happen to all those who are out there."

# Honest Questions for Personal Reflection

1. My favorite holiday is _____ because _____ .

2. One tradition or custom my family or church frequently observes that I really like is _____ . I like it because _____ .

3. One tradition or custom my family or church frequently observes that I really dislike is _____ . I dislike it because _____ .

# Honest Questions for Group Discussion

## Relate

1. Divide into two groups. Let one group prepare and present a brief speech on "Two Christian traditions that are really helpful" and the other group, "Two Christian traditions that do more harm than good." Then have the entire group discuss both speeches.

## Reflect

2. Read and discuss Mark 7:1-23.

- Verses 1-5. Why did the Pharisees and teachers of the law criticize Jesus' disciples? Why do you think ceremonial hand washing was so important to them?

- Verses 6-13. What is Jesus' main point here? Do you think people violate this principle today? If so, cite some specific examples.

- How can you tell the difference between a command of God and a human tradition?

- Verses 14-23. What is Jesus' main point? Do you think most people really understand the distinction between outward religious acts and inward spiritual commitment? Explain.

3. There's an old story about a grocer who was known for his honesty. To make sure he treated his customers fairly and never overcharged them, he carefully weighed items on a large scale that stood on the countertop. The grocer's son always admired the way his dad handled the business. After the older man died, the son was dismayed to discover that the scale had been calibrated incorrectly and its measurements were wrong. The old grocer had been unintentionally overcharging his customers for years!

- Should the grocer's son fix the defective scale, buy a new one, or continue to use the old one? Why?

- Would replacing the old scale dishonor his father who had used it for so many years? Explain.

- What do you think the grocer would want the son to do?

- How does this story relate to the religious traditions a family or ethnic group may hold dear?

4. Emiko observed, "I think Japanese Buddhists are like some Americans who go to church twice a year for Easter and Christmas. Whether they actually believe in Jesus' resurrection or not, it's a common practice." In your opinion, is this a fair comparison? Why or why not?

5. As time allows, assign and read the following Scriptures. Discu̇ some things these verses tell us about what God considers importa̧ and unimportant to our Christian faith.

Romans 14:1-18

Philippians 3:1-11

Colossians 2:6-8

Colossians 2:20-23

2 Thessalonians 2:13-17

1 Timothy 1:3-7

1 Timothy 4:1-10

2 Timothy 2:8-16

2 Timothy 2:22-24

1 Peter 1:18, 19

## Respond

6. Several steps were suggested for reaching out to someone l̇ Yoshi (p. 114). What do you think of those suggestions? Which any of them, have you used when talking with friends? What wo̧ you add to the list?

7. Focus your closing prayer time in two ways: first, on the freedom we enjoy in Christ (as described in Galatians 5:1 and Ephesians 3:12); and second, on a commitment to sharing with others about that freedom (see John 8:36; 2 Corinthians 3:17).

## Resources for Further Study

*Answering Islam: The Crescent in the Light of the Cross* by Norman L. Geisler and Abdul Saleeb (Grand Rapids, MI: Baker Books, 1993)

*Buddhism Through Christian Eyes* by Alex G. Smith (Littleton, CO: Overseas Missionary Fellowship, 2001). Excellent sixty-four-page booklet by a twenty-year missionary to Thailand.

*Handbook of Today's Religions* by Josh McDowell and Don Stewart (Nashville, TN: Thomas Nelson, revised edition 1996)

*How Now Shall We Live?* by Charles Colson and Nancy Pearcey (Wheaton, IL: Tyndale House, 1999)

*In Name Only: Tackling the Problem of Nominal Christianity* by Eddie Gibbs (Pasadena, CA: Fuller Seminary Press, 2000)

*Jesus Among Other Gods: The Absolute Claims of the Christian Message* by Ravi Zacharias (Nashville, TN: W Publishing Group / Thomas Nelson, 2002)

*The Universe Next Door: A Basic Worldview Catalog* by James W. Sire (Downers Grove, IL: InterVarsity Press, fifth edition 2009)

*Understanding World Religions* by George W. Braswell Jr. (Nashville, TN: Broadman & Holman Publishers, 1994)

Chapter

# Why Are There So Many Phony Christians?

**Mirror, mirror, on the wall, who's the Pharisee of us all?**
**a little boy, overheard by his mom**

Standing in an airport check-in line, I noticed a woman ahead of me holding two large boxes. When the attendant at the counter informed her that the boxes were too big to carry on, the woman flew into a rage. As the rest of us looked on, she complained loudly until the airline employee finally called for a supervisor, who verified that, indeed, the two boxes were too large to qualify as carry-ons.

I was the next passenger to approach the counter once the situation was resolved. I told the flustered-looking attendant, "It must be hard to stay calm when someone makes a scene like that."

She replied, "Yes, and do you know what was in those two boxes? Bibles! You wouldn't expect someone carrying boxes of Bibles to act like that, would you?"

Chagrined, I told her, "I'm sorry you were treated that way. Not everyone who believes the Bible acts like that."

Hypocrisy. Inconsistency. Problems like these have plagued God's people for centuries. And nobody likes the fake stuff.

• Real mashed potatoes taste better than instant ones.
• Live singing beats lip-syncing.

- A fake rose has no thorns . . . but also no fragrance.
- Baseball stadiums built with artificial turf are hot as a griddle and hard as concrete. Yes, natural grass has to be mowed, but it's the surface where baseball was meant to be played.

We prefer the authentic over the artificial, and so does the Lord. The prophet Jeremiah warned God's people, "Do not trust in deceptive words and say, 'This is the temple of the LORD, the temple of the LORD, the temple of the LORD!'"—as if merely showing up at the place of worship and repeating pious-sounding words over and over would make everything OK with God. God wanted the people to change their ways. "Will you steal and murder, commit adultery and perjury . . . and follow other gods," the Lord asked, "and then come and stand before me in this house, which bears my Name, and say, 'We are safe'—safe to do all these detestable things?" (Jeremiah 7:4, 9, 10).

It's sad when people who claim to know God gossip, cheat, lie, and hurt others just as much as the people who don't claim to know the Lord at all. What does it say to a watching world when a churchgoer talks big but acts small?

Our friends and neighbors can sniff out a phony a mile away. Researcher David Kinnaman observes, "The term 'hypocritical' has become fused to young people's experience with Christianity. Eighty-five percent of young outsiders [*his term for atheists, agnostics, non-Christians, the unchurched—all who look at Christianity from the outside*] have had sufficient exposure to Christians and churches that they conclude present-day Christianity is hypocritical."[1] Kinnaman's research uncovered a disturbing reality: "Among young outsiders, *84 percent* say they personally know at least one committed Christian. Yet just *15 percent* thought the lifestyles of those Christ followers were significantly different from the norm."[2]

Even allowing for some margin of error in surveys of this nature, it's still important for Christians to examine our own authenticity.

## Fighting the Good Fight of Fake

James wrote, "With the tongue we praise our Lord and Father, and with it we curse men, who have been made in God's likeness. . . . My brothers, this should not be" (James 3:9, 10). Peter said that believers should rid themselves of all kinds of hypocrisy (1 Peter 2:1). Paul wrote that Christians must "put off falsehood and speak truthfully" (Ephesians 4:25). The Lord wants us to be real.

A twenty-something man asked me, "Why do so many church services seem out of touch with real life? And why do so many churchgoers seem to play religious games instead of doing what the Bible says followers of Jesus should do?"

The young man further explained: "During my teen years, I didn't see any relevance or reality to the church at all outside of being a social club that you joined if you wanted to. Later, I began studying the Bible on my own and became very excited about what I was reading. It made sense to me that Jesus was the Son of God."

A note of frustration crept into his voice. "But then I had a hard time finding a church that practices what the Scripture requires. Scripture talks about people who were joyful. They would do things like praying all night for Simon Peter when he was in prison. I'd go into a church looking for real belief in Jesus and real worship. Instead, people would stand and sit and kneel, and say the same words over and over like they're supposed to—but there didn't seem to be any heart in it at all. It was different from what I was reading in Scripture that the church should be. Jesus said to feed the hungry and clothe the naked, and all I saw were churches worrying about budgets, flea markets, bazaars, bingo games, and casino nights. It didn't make sense to me. What I saw Scripture requiring was not what I saw in any churches around me. I thought, *Am I demanding too much of the church, or does it just not exist in the real world? Where can I find a church where people truly love Jesus?"*

Fake faith hurts and confuses people. Hypocritical Christians resemble the Major League umpire who was charged with shoplifting more than four thousand baseball cards from a retail store in Bakersfield,

California. A security officer at the store told police that he caught the ump putting seven boxes of cards, valued at about $144, into a brown paper bag.[3] It's common for an umpire to call out a base runner for trying to steal, but it's unacceptable for an umpire himself to be caught stealing! He's supposed to be the good guy, the authority figure, the one you respect even when you boo him. He's supposed to enforce the rules, not break them. It's disillusioning when someone who knows the rules fails to live by them.

A worker in the medical profession wrote a letter asking Dear Abby for advice on how to deal with a cranky coworker who constantly cursed and complained about the patients and the working conditions at her job. The writer, who signed her letter "Up to Here," was especially bothered by her coworker's claim to be a faithful Christian.

She wrote: "Her conversations are peppered with 'the Lord this' and 'the Lord that.' I have great difficulty understanding the inconsistencies between her professed faith and her actions. Although I am not an active member of my church, I wouldn't treat a dog the way this pious churchgoer treats people. . . . In my experience, I have usually found that those who thump their Bibles the loudest would benefit more by being thumped by them."[4]

Hypocrisy isn't the only sin, but it's a particularly egregious offense, for it undermines the credibility of the gospel when Christians don't walk what we talk.

So what should we say when a friend alleges that there's pretense and phoniness in the church? How can we defend the Christian faith against the charge that we're all a bunch of hypocrites?

## We Recognize That Hypocrisy Is a Serious Problem

It's undeniable that many Christians are guilty of hypocrisy. Sadly, the history of the church is filled with stories about people who failed to live consistent lifestyles of righteousness and faith. Catholic popes have insisted on celibacy for their priests, but sired children out of wedlock. Protestant preachers have used their pulpits to denounce

sexual immorality while secretly practicing the very sins they co
demned. Worshippers who sang "Praise the Lord" a few momen
ago at church yell "Same to you, fella!" as another driver cuts the
off in traffic during the drive hom
Some parents send their children
Sunday school, but in everyday li
they act as if God is irrelevant.

> The best argument for Christianity is Christians: their joy, their certainty, their completeness. But the strongest argument against Christianity is also Christians—when they are sombre and joyless, when they are self-righteous and smug in complacent consecration, when they are narrow and repressive, then Christianity dies a thousand deaths.[5]
>
> Sheldon Vanauken

Ugly church splits, caused by pe
sonality clashes and minor differen
es of opinion, have soured outside
and caused them to say, "ABC-
Anything But Church!"

Carl Ketcherside wrote that in t
early church, Christians "claimed
love each other and talked about J
sus; now they claim to love Jesus ar
talk about each other. In those da
all exerted an effort to exhort; now a
must be exhorted to exert an effort.

## Jesus Considered Hypocrisy a Serious Problem

Some of the strongest denunciations that ever came from the lips
Jesus were reserved for the religious leaders he said were like "whit
washed tombs, which look beautiful on the outside but on the insi
are full of dead men's bones and everything unclean" (Matthew 23:2;
Another time Jesus told about a Pharisee who went to the temple ar
offered a prayer filled with self-righteousness. "The Pharisee stood v
and prayed about himself: 'God, I thank you that I am not like oth
men—robbers, evildoers, adulterers—or even like this tax collecto
(Luke 18:11).

The problem is, hypocrisy is such a devious sin, we can read that sto
and think to ourselves, *I'm glad I'm not like that Pharisee*—and end u
just as self-righteous as he was!

The Lord's exposé of hypocrisy in Matthew 23 makes painful but worthwhile reading, because it paints a vivid portrait of religious phoniness. Here are nine lessons we find there:

1. Hypocrites do not practice what they preach (v. 3).
2. Hypocrites place on others heavy demands that they are unwilling to shoulder themselves (v. 4).
3. Hypocrites emphasize appearance rather than substance—"everything they do is done for men to see" (v. 5).

4. Hypocrites are preoccupied with recognition and status symbols. They want to impress others, receive public honors, and be called by prestigious titles (vv. 6-12).
5. Hypocrites hinder others from entering the kingdom of God (vv. 13-15).
6. Hypocrites highlight relatively unimportant things so others will notice and admire them, but overlook the big things (like justice, mercy, and faithfulness) that matter most in God's eyes (vv. 16-24).
7. Hypocrites look good on the outside but are corrupt on the inside (vv. 25-28).
8. Hypocrites bring harm to those who are truly trying to do God's will (vv. 29-36).
9. And yet, despite all their flaws, hypocrites are still the objects of Jesus' caring love. He's willing to embrace and help them, but first they must be willing to receive him (vv. 37-39).

## Messing Up Doesn't Make Someone a Hypocrite

The Greek word *hypokrites* (the root of our word *hypocrite*) referred to an actor—a performer in the theater who wore a mask or played the part of another person. Hypocrisy is playacting—but not in a good way! It's putting on "a false appearance," acting in a way that contradicts the person's stated beliefs.[7]

A person who makes a mistake should not be labeled a hypocrite.

In a way, it's odd that Christians would be accused of hypocrisy; every one who finds salvation in Christ accepts the painful reality that he (or she) is one of the "all" in "all have sinned and fall short of the glory of God (Romans 3:23). We agree with the apostle John who wrote, "If we claim to be without sin, we deceive ourselves and the truth is not in us" (1 John 1:8)

During a debate, Abraham Lincoln's opponent referred to him as "two-faced." Lincoln responded, "I leave it to you, my audience: If I were two-faced, would I be wearing this one?"[8]

How can Christians be considered phonies when we openly acknowledge we are sinners? Part of becoming a Christian is facing up to our own sin in genuine repentance. We accept the humbling fact that we can't make things right with God through our own human effort. We are saved through the undeserved kindness of God expressed to us through the sacrificial death of his Son. "It is by grace you have been saved (Ephesians 2:8-10).

When we are baptized into Christ (Acts 2:38; Galatians 3:27), we are not declaring to the world that we are graduates of the Ain't-I-Perfect School of Theology. We are like newborn babies, dependent on our heavenly Father, eager to grow in his grace. Messing up doesn't make us hypocrites. We trust in God's blessed assurance that "if we confess our sins, he is faithful and just and will forgive us our sins and purify us from all unrighteousness" (1 John 1:9).

## Christians Aren't the Only Hypocrites

When it comes to hypocrisy, Christians don't have a corner on the market.

- What about wealthy politicians who give less than 2 percent of their income to charity but criticize the rich in order to gain the votes of the poor?
- What about employees who bitterly criticize the boss when he's not around but pretend to show respect when he's in the room?

- What about the guy who publicly decries racism but privately despises the immigrants who moved into his neighborhood?
- What about alcohol manufacturers who spend millions to convince young people it's cool to drink with their friends, then sponsor pious-sounding commercials that lecture us about drunk driving?
- What about political activists who arrive in gas-guzzling limousines at a conference to discuss the environment, and during the conference their trash cans overflow with photocopied materials, throwaway plates, aluminum cans, and plastic utensils?

People who say one thing but act another way show up in all walks of life.

## Sincere Christians Are on the Right Road

Rubel Shelly writes, "My role as a 'Christian apologist' . . . does not obligate me to defend any particular expression of Christian faith within a certain denomination or sect. . . . Neither am I committed to defend the wicked things that people have done in the name of Christianity through the centuries—whether the Spanish Inquisition or a personal sin in my life. The truth or falsity of Christian faith is a separate issue from the faithfulness or unfaithfulness of its adherents in practicing it."[9]

The road toward God is the right road.

It's true that some hypocrites fake their faith because they don't really believe in the first place. Not everyone who claims to be a Christian is truly following Christ. Jesus compared the kingdom of Heaven to a field where weeds take root among the wheat and both kinds of plants grow together until the harvest (the final judgment), when God separates his true followers from the false followers (Matthew 13:24-30, 36-43).

However, other people sincerely believe in Christ. Their actions don't totally line up with their beliefs, but it's because their faith is still immature and undeveloped. We don't expect ten-year-olds to play the piano or serve a tennis ball as well as an experienced pianist or tennis player who's been practicing much longer. Likewise, we shouldn't expect a new or unseasoned believer to demonstrate spiritual maturity that takes years to develop.

Holiness (what theologians call sanctification) is both a state and a process. When we accept Christ as Savior, we become "holy people"—distinct, pure, set apart in a special state of holiness in God's eyes—not because of our own merits but because we are in Christ. As soon as we are saved, we enter a process of holiness in which the Holy Spirit helps us grow more and more like Christ. Thus, Peter could call Christians "a holy nation" while also urging, "Be holy in all you do" (1 Peter 2:9; 1:15). As another Bible author puts it, "By one sacrifice [Jesus] has made perfect forever those who are being made holy" (Hebrews 10:14).

We should not try to reduce God's demands by adopting an easy believe-ism that waters down what the Lord expects of us. Nor should we acknowledge that God's standards are high while pretending that we are living at a higher level than we actually have attained.[10]

We should be honest about our imperfections while we grow in godliness with the help of the Holy Spirit. Even the great apostle Paul admitted that he had not already been made perfect, but he was determined to "press on toward the goal" (Philippians 3:12-14). That's why he told Christians to "continue to work out your salvation with fear and trembling" (2:12). As we grow spiritually, our outward actions and inner character should line up more and more with the Savior's holiness (see 2 Peter 1:5-11).

Thoughtful Christians recognize their need to struggle against hypocrisy. Christian leaders who have walked with the Lord a long time may wrestle honestly with their own shortcomings but don't want to shortchange the Lord's standards. R. C. Sproul points out that many of a sincere minister's sermons "are born out of the minister's own personal struggles. . . . To preach at a higher level than you perform is not hypocrisy. To claim a higher level of performance than you have attained is hypocrisy."[11]

## I'm Responsible for Me

If some people in the church are faking it, my faith doesn't have to be phony too.

If a well-known church leader turns out to be a fraud, that doesn't mean I get a free pass for ignoring God myself.

The hypocrisy of other people doesn't reduce or eliminate my own accountability to God. On Judgment Day it won't do any good to point a finger at others and say, "They didn't live up to what they professed." The Bible says, "Each of us will give an account of himself to God" (Romans 14:12). I'm responsible for me.

It's foolish to conclude that because a few doctors are quacks, I will never take any form of medicine. By refusing medical treatment, I wouldn't get back at the quacks; I would only hurt myself! It's equally foolish to conclude that because some Christians are phonies, God is unworthy of our trust and the church he set up is irrelevant. By refusing to participate in the church, I don't punish the hypocrites; I only hurt myself.

Even if any given local church *were* full of hypocrites, that still wouldn't excuse each of us from our own personal accountability to God.

"It's important to challenge ourselves," a friend of mine observed. "A lot of our pushing God away and pushing the church away is deeper than just saying what's wrong with 'them.' Maybe the real issue is how I feel about myself and not how I feel about the church. There needs to be some healthy self-examination as well."

> Christianity has not been tried and found wanting; it has been found difficult and not tried.[12]
>
> G. K. Chesterton

## A Healthy Church Is Beautiful

Let's be honest all the way. The church—those flawed but forgiven believers all over the world—at its best is a lovely thing with strengths and positive contributions. Even with its shortcomings, the church deserves honor and respect, because God describes the church with terms like these:

- people of God (1 Peter 2:9, 10; Titus 2:14)
- called of God (Romans 8:30; 2 Peter 1:10; Revelation 17:14)
- household, or family, of God (Ephesians 2:19; 1 Timothy 3:15; Galatians 6:10)
- kingdom of God (Romans 14:17; Colossians 1:13)
- flock of God (Acts 20:28)
- God's farm (field), building, temple (1 Corinthians 3:9-17)

God's people are the branches and Jesus is the vine (John 15:1-6). We are the body and Christ is the head (Ephesians 1:22, 23; 4:11-16). We are "living stones" and he is the "living Stone," the "cornerstone," the foundation of God's temple (1 Peter 2:4-6). The church is the bride; he is the bridegroom (Ephesians 5:22, 23; Revelation 19:7). We are the sheep; he is the shepherd (John 10:1-18). He is the light of the world (John 8:12), and we reflect his light to others (Matthew 5:14).

Retired preacher Robert Shannon observes:

The church may not be as good as God intended, but she is not as bad as her critics suppose. The church where I preach is full of hypocrites. I am glad. I welcome them. The church is the only place where a hypocrite is welcome. If the church doesn't help them, no one else will. Saying the church is full of hypocrites is like saying the hospital is full of sick people. Of course it is. Where else can sick people go? It is like saying Alcoholics Anonymous is full of alcoholics. Of course it is. Where did the idea come from that church membership is a badge of moral perfection, that even church attendance is a symbol of spiritual purity? Churches are hospitals for sinners—not clubs for saints. The church is not made up of good people, but people trying to be good.[13]

If Goldilocks had been searching for a church instead of porridge, she would have learned that some congregations seem too hard, some too soft, some too hot, some too cold. Where could she have found a church that was just right? How about this one:

- a church built on the foundation of Christ as Lord and Savior
- a church that proclaimed the good news and joyfully baptized those who believed
- a church where young and old met together consistently for prayer, fellowship, teaching, and Communion
- a church where people loved each other, met one another's needs, and worshipped together in unity
- a church that grew spontaneously because of a Holy Spirit-engendered genuineness no one could deny or quench

That is the kind of church we see in Acts 2:36-47. Although we may not reproduce it perfectly today, can't we strive to be that kind of church? And can't we share that intent with our unbelieving friends?

We can't give up on the church! It's not just a man-made, optional institution. Christ calls it "my church" (Matthew 16:18). He loves the church and died for it (Ephesians 5:25). Before Paul became a follower of Christ, he had "persecuted the church" (Galatians 1:13); but at the time, Jesus took it personally, saying that Paul was persecuting Jesus himself (Acts 9:4).

Someone has said, "The world at its worst needs the church at its best." Constant fault finding leads nowhere. Instead, let's do whatever we can to make the church the best it can be.

## Authentic Faith *Does* Exist

The title of this chapter asks, "Why are there so many phony Christians?"

We might ask back: "*Are* there?"

The bad guys make the news, for sure. And some folks who've had a negative experience with one person in a church of three hundred members may say in frustration, "The people in that church are hypocrites!"

Such statements get passed along, with few people bothering to find out that there weren't three hundred hypocrites, just one.

If I have to explain why some Christians are fake, then a skeptic should have to explain why so many Christians demonstrate a faith that's real, dynamic, life changing—even inspirational.

Consider what happened to Darrell Thompson and his wife, Maria.[14] A military veteran who served twenty-two years in the Marines and the Air Force Reserves, Darrell is an experienced aircraft mechanic and engineer employed now by a steel manufacturer in northeast Ohio. On an unseasonably warm, sunny day in November 2010, Maria went to her job while Darrell stayed home to work in the back woods of their property.

After gathering up some brush and trash and adding kerosene to help it burn, Darrell sensed an eerie feeling of danger; so to be extra safe, he postponed lighting the match and took the kerosene can back to the garage. Returning to the woods, he lit the match, not realizing he was surrounded by a pocket of odorless methane gas. (Cow manure and dead brush from surrounding farms had created what amounted to an invisible bomb.)

When Darrell lit the match, he heard a loud *whooshing* sound and found himself surrounded by fire. He could feel his ears and hair burning. Amid his shock, he heard a voice telling him to move. Running to a nearby creek, he dunked his head into the mud and water and then screamed for help. Neighbors heard and called the fire department, but by now Darrell was stuck in mud up to his waist and surrounded by smoke.

Maria says, "My neighbor called me, and I rushed home to find Darrell in the ambulance. I remember the skin on both his arms hanging like onion peels. He was burned on 85 percent of his body. His back had second-degree burns, but the rest were third-degree burns that would require skin grafts. He was in a hospital-induced coma for eight weeks and on a ventilator."

Maria saw Darrell through about twenty surgeries. "They had to cover his skin with temporary skin. They used pig and cadaver skin to ensure he would not get infections; they used his own unburned skin to graft some parts."

I met Darrell and Maria a year after the accident and was amazed by the undeniable strength of their faith. If any experience would test a person's commitment to God, surely it would be a painful, random accident like the one they endured.

Yet here's how Maria described their reaction: "It was a very trying time for us, but as I prayed and cried out to God, never did I feel angry or blame God for this accident. I felt assured that God was with us through the ordeal. Our ministers and church family immediately started a prayer chain and a prayer vigil for Darrell, and they ministered to me as well. It was a comfort as the love of God poured out. I felt assured that Darrell was going to be OK, even during his worst times. We are so thankful for the gift of life."

After intensive therapy and support from the Akron Children's Hospital Burn Unit, Darrell has gone back to work six days a week. Maria says, "He is not 100 percent healed—he's still in pain, still taking medication, still receiving therapy—but by God's grace he is back working at his job. Thanks be to God!"

It's easy to point out the flaws of fake believers, but how do you explain the faith displayed by sincere Christians like Darrell and Maria Thompson? Such stories exist by the thousands.

My dad farmed his land and served his community throughout his life. In his final years he suffered intensely from diabetic neuropathy that weakened his once-strong body and caused excruciating pain. Yet his faith remained strong till the day he died, and so did his love for my mother (to whom he was happily married for nearly sixty-four years). I can testify that his faith was genuine.

Joni Eareckson Tada became a quadriplegic at age seventeen but, decades later, still manages to write books, create art, and run an international ministry for the disabled.[15] She loves the Lord. Who would dare to suggest that her faith is phony?

Walk into just about any gathering of Christians and listen to their stories. You will discover individuals who have turned their losses into pluses, victims who founded ministries to help other victims, and sincere believers who became Christians because they saw someone else's life dramatically changed through Jesus. You will discover people familiar with radiation and chemotherapy who believe that "the big C" means Christ, not cancer. You will find givers who are amazingly generous because they are so grateful for God's grace, and survivors who miss their deceased loved ones but still trust in the Lord and refuse to "grieve like the rest of men, who have no hope" (1 Thessalonians 4:13). You will discover vibrant young people filled with undeniable passion for God, and wise old saints whose lives bear quiet testimony to the reality of faith.

Are all these believers a bunch of hypocrites? I don't think so.

## We Know Someone Who *Is* Perfect

If you identify some inconsistency in the life of any Christian, you haven't destroyed the credibility of God, his church, or the good news of Jesus Christ. Don't look only at Christians; look at Christ!

- Jesus didn't say, "Pretend that you're perfect." He said, "Follow me" (Mark 2:14; Luke 18:22).
- He never said, "Do as I say, not as I do." He said, "I have set you an example that you should do as I have done for you" (John 13:15).
- The apostle Paul didn't say, "Fall in line and fake it." He said, "Follow my example, as I follow the example of Christ" (1 Corinthians 11:1).
- The apostle Peter had his personal ups and downs, but in the end he realized that Jesus was the real deal. He said, "To this you were called, because Christ suffered for you, leaving you an example, that you should follow in his steps. 'He committed no sin, and no deceit was found in his mouth'" (1 Peter 2:21, 22).

The head of the church is no hypocrite. Jesus Christ never sinned, never lied, never pretended to be something he is not. We are imperfect followers of a perfect Lord. No matter how closely you look at him, you'll never find anything phony about Jesus Christ.

# Honest Questions for Personal Reflection

1. Recall some examples of hypocrisy you've seen in current ever that made the news. What makes the people or situations so hypocritica

2. Has anyone ever accused you of being a hypocrite? If so, do y think the accusation was valid? Why or why not?

# Honest Questions for Group Discussion

## Relate

1. Each member can tell the group about one of the following:

- the outfit you wore to the last costume party you attended
- a character you once portrayed in a school play
- a famous person or cartoon character you can imitate

2. Each member will need two index cards and a pencil. On o of the cards, each person should write a true but little-known fa about himself. On the other card, each person should write a "p tend fact"—something that isn't true—about himself. The group lead should shuffle the cards and read them aloud. The group can guess w wrote the information and whether the information is true or false.

## Reflect

3. Have you ever felt disappointed by a Christian whose actions were inconsistent with what he or she claimed to believe? How did you deal with your disappointment?

4. Has anyone ever told you that the church is "full of hypocrites"? How did you respond? Now, having read this chapter, might you respond differently? How?

5. (or do the variation in question 6) Read and discuss the following portions of Jesus' exposé of hypocrisy recorded in Matthew 23.

• Verses 1-15. What did these people do that was inconsistent with their professed beliefs? How did their actions harm other people?

• Verses 25-28. How would you describe the tone of Jesus' words? Does this surprise you? Why or why not?

• Verse 37. After all Jesus had said about the hypocrites, why did he suddenly sound so eager to be kind to them?

6. (a variation of question 5) If you have a large group, divide into smaller groups of two or three people each. Provide pencil and paper to one person in each group, the "writer." Each group should read and discuss one of the following sections of Matthew 23 and write their own paraphrase of it, expressing in contemporary words what Jesus might say to hypocrites today. Then bring the large group back together and read what's been written.

- Verses 1-4
- Verses 5-12
- Verses 13-22
- Verses 23-28
- Verses 29-33

7. Read Acts 2:42-47. What was the New Testament church like in its earliest days? Is it realistic to think that a church could be like that today? Why or why not?

## Respond

8. What practical steps could you take to make the worship of God and the personal relationships in your church more authentic?

9. Open group prayer time with silent prayer for individuals to ask the Lord to forgive any personal hypocrisy they've become aware of. The leader can close with an audible prayer for the Lord's help as each member tries to make his or her faith real in every way.

# Resources for Further Study

*Authentic Christianity* by Ray C. Stedman (Grand Rapids, MI: Discovery House Publishers, 1996)

*Being the Body: A New Call for the Church to be Light in the Darkness* by Charles Colson and Ellen Vaughn (Nashville, TN: W Publishing Group / Nelson, 2003)

*Eats with Sinners* by Arron Chambers (Cincinnati, OH: Standard Publishing, 2009). "A biblical model for evangelism—building relationships like Jesus did." Can be used as a small group study.

*Unchristian: What a New Generation Really Thinks About Christianity . . . and Why It Matters* by David Kinnaman and Gabe Lyons (Grand Rapids, MI: Baker Books, 2007)

*Unnamed: Unsuspecting Heroes Singled Out by God* by Chris Travis (Cincinnati, OH: Standard Publishing, 2010). Unlikely Bible characters whose "adventures reveal the kind of lasting impact that God intends each of us to have." (*Unnamed Group Member Discussion Guide* also available.)

## Chapter 8

# Why Are Christians So Intolerant?

**We should note this curious mark of our own age: the only absolute allowed is the absolute insistence that there is no absolute.**
**Francis Schaeffer**

Natalie started attending the church I led in New York. A quiet, pleasant person, she seemed to appreciate the biblical teaching and friendly atmosphere she found in our church. After some time, she dropped by my office one day. She said, "I like this church very much, but from listening to the messages each week, I get the impression that you think it's necessary to believe in Jesus Christ in order to go to Heaven. That sounds awfully intolerant to me."

"We do believe it's necessary to trust and obey Jesus," I replied, "but not because we're intolerant or trying to exclude anyone. It's just that we want to be faithful to Jesus' own words when he said, 'I am the way and the truth and the life. No one comes to the Father except through me'" (John 14:6).

She thanked me for my honesty and then informed me, "If that's the case, this isn't the church for me."

Our conversation had been sincere and respectful, and I attempted to pursue it further; but she politely said good-bye and left. I saw her a few weeks later in a grocery store and we exchanged friendly greetings, but she was true to her word. She never came to our church again.

I feel sad when I recall my encounter with Natalie, but I know that her discomfort with Jesus' truth claims is not unusual. According to a 2011 Barna Research poll, 43 percent of Americans think "it doesn't matter what religious faith you follow because they all teach the same lessons," and 50 percent believe that "all people are eventually saved or accepted by God no matter what they do."[1]

Remember Pat, who in chapter 3 had said, "If you think of God as a room, Christians believe there is only one door into the room and Christianity is it"? She further explained, "To me, this invalidates genuine revelatory experiences that others have encountered in other belief systems." She's willing to agree that Christianity is one "door," but not the only one.

## Three Troublesome Trends

Natalie, Pat, and many others struggle with the issue of tolerance because, whether they realize it or not, they have been deeply affected by postmodern philosophies widespread in our culture. Ravi Zacharias summarizes the situation as follows:

1. Philosophy has moved to the existential.
2. Art has moved to the sensual.
3. Religion has moved to the mystical.
4. Education has moved to the skeptical.
5. The individual has moved to the transcendental ("that is, he is his own divine being").[2]

Here are three current trends that are particularly troublesome: relativism, pluralism, and universalism.

## 1. Relativism

Our culture suffers from a serious case of truth decay. Most Americans do not believe in absolute truth. Surveys conducted by Barna Research found that by a three-to-one margin, adult Americans said, "Truth is always relative to the person and their situation." Among teenagers,

83 percent said, "Moral truth depends on the circumstances," and only 6 percent believe that moral truth is absolute.[3]

From the relativist's point of view, spiritual journeys and moral choices depend completely on each individual's situation and perspective. Our postmodern neighbors are suspicious of religious truth claims and reluctant to receive any message that sounds preachy, narrow, or intolerant. The one Bible verse most people can quote? "Do not judge, or you too will be judged" (Matthew 7:1).

Culture analyst David Kinnaman cites surveys indicating that "nearly nine out of ten [non-Christians] . . . said that the term *judgmental* accurately describes present-day Christianity."[4] According to Kinnaman, there are two reasons today's young adults find it particularly difficult to swallow judgmental attitudes:

> First, they are insightful about people's motives. They have been the target of endless lectures, sermons, marketing, and advertisement. If you bring up unsolicited advice, they mistrust your motives. They wonder what's in it for you when you offer your opinion. Second, the new generations are increasingly resistant to simplistic, black-and-white views of the world. . . . They esteem context, ambiguity, and tension. Often judgmental attitudes come across as overly simplified, old-fashioned, and out of step with their diverse world.[5]

## 2. Pluralism

*Pluralism* is defined as "a situation in which people of different social classes, religions, races, etc., are together in a society but continue to have their different traditions and interests."[6] Our Western culture sees a growing diversity and values toleration of this diversity. It's even engraved on our coins and bills: *e pluribus unum*—"out of the many, one." Christians gladly embrace pluralism in this sense, for Christianity and other faiths have flourished in America where various ethnic groups find freedom to live and worship as they choose.

**Visit us at lamag.com**

# BUSINESS REPLY MAIL

FIRST-CLASS MAIL    PERMIT NO. 459    FLAGLER BEACH, FL

POSTAGE WILL BE PAID BY ADDRESSEE

LOS ANGELES MAGAZINE
PO BOX 421929
PALM COAST FL 32142-7695

# Los Angeles
### MAGAZINE

*Summer Gift Savings*

*Buy one* subscription for yourself, *Get one* gift to give for **FREE!**
That's 2 one-year subscriptions for just $20!

Perfect for mom, dad, grads, or just because!

## YOUR SUBSCRIPTION

NAME

ADDRESS

CITY                    STATE        ZIP

E-MAIL Please e-mail me new features and offers from *Los Angeles* magazine.

## GIFT SUBSCRIPTION

NAME

ADDRESS

CITY                    STATE        ZIP

Please list additional gifts on separate sheets of paper ($10 each).

☐ PAYMENT ENCLOSED        ☐ PLEASE BILL ME

Please allow 6 weeks for delivery. Offer valid for new U.S. orders only. Cost if only one subscription ordered is $12.

R307SB

But in a postmodern world, pluralism has a new wrinkle. Now, many understand pluralism to mean that no belief system can claim to be superior. While there have always been many religions to choose from, our neighbors now find themselves at a spiritual smorgasbord where all "soul food" is considered equally satisfying. John Lennon reflected this attitude when he said, "I believe that what people call God is something in all of us. I believe that what Jesus and Mohammed and Buddha and all the rest said was right. It's just that the translations have gone wrong."[7]

Hamish Taylor leads a ministry called Rechurch in New Zealand. [8] He says:

> I'm talking with a young man who has been dancing around the idea of faith for years. His girlfriend is a Hindu. He respects her morals and her stable life. She has been open to talking about Christianity, but her attitude is, "Any faith is good faith."
>
> I have another friend—a refugee from Afghanistan—who has seen all sorts of terrible things done in the name of religion. He has a Muslim family but describes himself as "a free man" with no religion. He says that all religions are the same.
>
> Another lady had all sorts of questions that acted as barriers to her becoming a Christian, such as, "If Jesus is the only way to God, what happens to those remote tribes that never heard of him?"

This skewed form of pluralism views all religious beliefs as equally valid (or invalid)—but in the process it does a disservice to all faiths. Anyone who examines different religions closely will discover profound differences in their teachings about God and the way to salvation. They're not all the same.

## 3. Universalism

The philosophy of universalism has become deeply imbedded in the psyche of our generation. The idea that one must believe in Jesus Christ to be saved sounds, to postmodern ears, antiquated and narrow beyond belief. According to Jesus, the broad road leads to destruction and the narrow road leads to life (Matthew 7:13, 14), but universalists say the wide road is the right road and all people, no matter how unfaithful and disobedient, eventually will be saved. They emphasize God's love and mercy but minimize his wrath and righteousness. They ignore the concept of Hell and assume that all who die will go to Heaven regardless of their beliefs. Some universalists reject the Bible entirely as an authoritative standard, while others use Scripture to support their position, citing passages like 1 Timothy 2:3, 4 ("God . . . wants all men to be saved").

Universalism's popularity comes as no surprise. If believers and unbelievers alike will experience salvation, why be concerned about new birth, holy living, or sound doctrine? Why risk offending anyone by speaking about Jesus Christ? Why draw any religious lines in the sand? Universalism is a live-and-let-live philosophy, a religion of few demands.

Many who don't call themselves universalists adopt the philosophy nonetheless and express it with statements like these:

- "Oh well, we're all headed to the same place."
- "Don't be so narrow-minded. Christianity is no better than any other faith."
- "A loving God would never condemn anyone."
- "Sincerity is all that matters."
- "There may be a main road to Heaven, but a lot of service roads connect to it."

Remember, once we have concluded that the Bible is true, as discussed in chapter 2, we need to let the Bible itself have the last word; and biblically speaking, there are many problems with universalism:

- It dampens our appreciation for God's grace. If everyone is going to be saved anyway, what's the big deal about being rescued from sin?

- It steals our zeal for evangelism. In the book of Acts, the church grew because Spirit-led believers preached passionately and lived sacrificially. They believed eternal life hung in the balance and salvation could be found in Christ alone.
- It weakens our understanding of the church's purpose. Jesus not only said, "Whoever believes and is baptized will be saved"; he also said, "Whoever does not believe will be condemned" (Mark 16:16). Ambiguity about our message produces apathy toward our mission. Universalism attacks the nerve center of the body of Christ, paralyzing outreach efforts and lulling believers into selfishness, indifference, and inactivity.
- It contradicts the direct teaching of Jesus. He was asked, "Lord, are only a few people going to be saved?" He responded, "Make every effort to enter through the narrow door, because many, I tell you, will try to enter and will not be able to" (Luke 13:23, 24).

Ultimate judgment is God's prerogative, not ours. Our job isn't to consign others to Hell, but neither do we have the right to pronounce someone "saved" simply because he "seems saved" to us. Nor is it our job to insist on man-made rules and opinions that make that "narrow door" narrower. Instead, we need to focus on and proclaim what God has plainly revealed—even when it's unpopular—and trust him with what we don't know.

## Tolerance: Let's Understand It

To *tolerate* means "to endure" or "to put up with" something; "to endure or resist the action of [something] without serious side effects or discomfort."[9] If you drink a lot of coffee, your body will build up a tolerance to caffeine. If you live in a tropical climate, you develop a tolerance to hot weather.

Since the United States began, it has followed a policy of toleration by allowing citizens to express and follow a wide variety of religious and political beliefs without hindrance by the government. The First Amendment to the United States Constitution guarantees this right: "Congress shall make no law respecting an establishment of religion, or prohibiting the free exercise thereof." (Thomas Jefferson famously referred to this amendment in an 1802 letter to the Danbury Baptist Association, mentioning what he called "a wall of separation between church and State.")[10] The concept of religious tolerance is deeply embedded in the American way of life. In practice, tolerance looks like this:

- disagreeing strongly with someone's ideas but still treating him with respect
- understanding your own convictions and holding firmly to them, while allowing others to explain and defend their points of view and practice their faith without interference
- Democrats, Republicans, and Independents working together in unity in the church despite their political differences
- a Jewish rabbi and a Christian minister talking amiably about their religious differences while they work on a community project together

On the other hand, intolerance looks like this:

- NFL quarterback Tim Tebow being ridiculed for his open expression of his Christian faith
- a Christian being labeled homophobic because he believes the Bible's teaching on homosexual behavior
- members of a church picketing the funerals of American military personnel with signs that say, "Thank God for dead soldiers"
- a Christian mocking a devout Muslim coworker by referring to him as a terrorist

The problem is, many today seem to define *tolerance* as "accepting everyone's viewpoints as equally valid." While every person has the right to hold a personal opinion, that doesn't mean every opinion actually corresponds to reality.

Give me $100 and send me to the local supermarket, and I'm free to purchase a wide variety of items. But not everything I can purchase possesses equal nutritional value. I could use my money to purchase ice cream or broccoli or canned soup . . . I'm free to purchase whatever I want, but some things are good for me to eat; others are not. (And it's kind, not "intolerant," for another customer in the soup aisle to care enough to say, "Excuse me, but did you know there are some really good soups here that don't contain additives?") As an American citizen I enjoy great freedom to believe and practice whatever faith I choose, but that doesn't mean every religious option is equally nourishing to my soul. (And it's kind, not "intolerant," for someone to care enough to caution me against going down a dangerous path.)

> If all ideas are equally valid, as postmodernism insists, then no idea is really worth our allegiance; nothing is worth living or dying for—or even arguing about.[11]
>
> Charles Colson

Christian writer Paul Copan explains, "Contrary to popular definitions, true tolerance means 'putting up with error'—not 'being accepting of all views.' We don't tolerate what we enjoy or approve of. . . . By definition, what we tolerate is what we disapprove of or what we believe to be false and erroneous."[12] Copan continues, "If disagreement didn't exist, then tolerance would be unnecessary."[13]

Copan recommends that if someone accuses you of being intolerant, you should ask him to clarify what he means by using that term. "If by 'tolerance' the person means 'accepting all views as true,'" Copan says, "then you can say, 'You don't accept *my* view as true. Are you being intolerant?'"[14] John F. Kennedy put it this way: "Tolerance implies no lack of commitment to one's own beliefs. Rather it condemns the oppression or persecution of others."[15]

Excessive tolerance leads to permissiveness—allowing, endorsing, and encouraging any behavior at all, including destructive ones. At the other extreme, excessive intolerance leads to persecution—rejecting and punishing anyone who disagrees with our position, trying to force him to accept our views. Instead of either extreme (permissiveness or persecution), Christians ought to pursue the healthy middle ground of persuasion. We don't try to force anyone to accept God's standards, but we believe the truth has the power to change minds and hearts.[16]

Actually, it's odd that Christians would be considered intolerant; for unlike many religious systems that are tied to a specific ethnic group, Christianity says God loves all people equally (John 3:16), invites everyone to come to him through Christ (Revelation 22:17), and wants to unite us in love regardless of our ethnic or cultural backgrounds (Colossians 3:11-14). Centuries before it was popular to be inclusive, Jesus started a church in which everyone has equal standing, where "there is neither Jew nor [Gentile], slave nor free, male nor female, for you are all one in Christ Jesus" (Galatians 3:26-28). What's intolerant about *that*?

## Who's Being Narrow-Minded?

Timothy Keller writes:

Skeptics believe that *any* exclusive claims to a superior knowledge of spiritual reality cannot be true. But this objection is itself a religious belief. It assumes God is unknowable, or that God is loving but not wrathful, or that God is an impersonal force rather than a person who speaks in Scripture. All of these are unprovable faith assumptions. In addition, their proponents believe they have a superior way to view things. They believe the world would be a better place if everyone dropped the traditional religions' views of

God and truth and adopted theirs. Therefore, their view is also an "exclusive" claim about the nature of spiritual reality. If all such views are to be discouraged, this one should be as well. If it is not narrow to hold this view, then there is nothing inherently narrow about holding to traditional religious beliefs.[17]

Christians aren't trying to make our faith unreasonably exclusive. We're trying to be consistent with the teachings of Jesus, who claimed to be the only way to the Father (John 14:6; 1 Timothy 2:5). The Bible plainly indicates these six things:

1. There is one true God, and he alone is the author of salvation. "I, even I, am the LORD, and apart from me there is no Savior" (Isaiah 43:11).
2. Jesus Christ is God's "one and only Son" (John 3:16). At the cross and the empty tomb, he accomplished what only he could do.
3. We can't earn eternal life by good behavior. Salvation is a gift graciously bestowed by God, which we must receive by faith (Ephesians 2:8-10).
4. Judgment, Heaven, and Hell are real. Jesus said, "A time is coming when all who are in their graves will hear his voice and come out—those who have done good will rise to live, and those who have done evil will rise to be condemned" (John 5:28, 29).
5. Each of us has a personal responsibility to accept God's gift of salvation. God forces himself on no one, but says, "Whoever is thirsty, let him come; and whoever wishes, let him take the free gift of the water of life" (Revelation 22:17).
6. We serve a caring God who "is patient . . . not wanting anyone to perish, but everyone to come to repentance" (2 Peter 3:9)—a God who "so loved the world," whose Son came

to rescue us from condemnation (John 3:16, 17). We can share this message of hope without being condescending or holier-than-thou.

## Truth: Let's Face It

When I was growing up, my parents expected me to be honest. So when a baseball crashed through the dining room window, I told them the truth: "My brother threw it!"

My parents said, "Don't jump on the bed." But one day my brothers and I were horsing around, wrestling on the bed. When all three of us crash-landed onto the bed at the same time, the old, wooden frame split right down the side. It was hard for my dad to face the truth that we'd done such a thing. He was still angry later that week when we got into our cars and drove back to college!

I once conducted my own informal survey about truth. I asked people to complete the sentence, "It's hard to tell the truth when . . ." Nearly two hundred people responded, ranging from age four to age seventy-nine. Some of their responses were amusing: It's hard to tell the truth . . .

- when you return from a fishing trip. (male, age 49)
- when someone asks your age and weight. (female, age 49— *presumably!*)
- when your mouth is full. (male, age 5)

Other responses were quite insightful: It's hard to tell the truth . . .

- when you want to fit in. (female, age 13)
- when you don't know what the truth is. (male, age 22)
- when people are going to laugh at me. (female, age 9)
- when the truth isn't the answer people want to hear. (male, age 19)
- when my family members don't agree with my Christianity. (female, age 70)

Sometimes it's hard to tell the truth. But if there's anything our world needs today, it's truth. God desires that we have truth at the core of our being (see Psalm 51:6). Dozens of times in the Gospels Jesus said, "I tell you the truth" (or as the *King James Version* puts it, "Verily, verily, I say unto thee"; John 3:11, for example). Jesus rebuked the religious leaders who devalued the truth by their hypocrisy. But to those who believed in him, he said, "If you hold to my teaching, you are really my disciples. Then you will know the truth, and the truth will set you free" (John 8:31, 32).

When we engage in conversation with our friends, what should we say about truth?

## Truth is real

Jesus says we can know truth. There was a time in America when hardly anyone disputed that truth does in fact exist. Where I grew up, right and wrong were pretty clear-cut. Even my high school colors were black and white. (Really!) People didn't always agree, but they generally assumed that truth was real and you could know it.

Today our culture has sacrificed truth on the altar of tolerance. But you can't erase the lines on the court and take down the goal, then try to play basketball. You can't remove the steering wheel, the speedometer, and the brake pedal, then try to drive a car. In many other areas of life, truth is narrow. Why not in matters of faith? Why wouldn't the God who created an orderly universe ask us to respond to him within certain prescribed limits?

A former student of mine, Michael Tolle, took a university class in which he was assigned to a discussion group led by one of that university's top professors.[18] Michael recalls:

The professor told us about two scientists who were debating whether the sun revolved around the earth or the earth revolved around the sun. They decided to settle their disagreement by watching the sunrise together. So the next morning the two men met at a park bench and watched the sunrise. As the sun finished breaking off the horizon, the men looked at each other and simultaneously shouted, *"See!?"*

The professor explained that the point of the illustration was to get members of our discussion group to recognize that we can all look at the same thing and see something different, based on our individual points of view—so we should be open to everyone's opinion.

But I saw another side to that illustration, so I raised my hand. I told the professor, "I understand that there were different viewpoints. But the fact is, the guy who thought the earth revolved around the sun was *right!*"

In a confused world where more and more people "call evil good and good evil," "put darkness for light and light for darkness," and "put bitter for sweet and sweet for bitter" (Isaiah 5:20), facts are still facts, and not every option is a correct one—or even a good one.

## Truth is written

God has made his truth known through Scripture.

When my wife, Candy, was studying to be a registered nurse, she took a class on medical ethics during which the teacher said that in most situations there are no certain truths, no right and wrong answers. Funny. They didn't say that in Candy's chemistry class, or microbiology, or anatomy and physiology. In those classes, the professors were very *picky* about truth! They made her memorize countless facts about medicines and hospital procedures. They insisted she learn the truth about bones, blood, organs, nerves . . . because a patient's well-being would be at stake. Candy was expected to study what the experts had written about those things.

God designed our physical bodies to work in certain ways. Doesn't it make sense that he would also reveal how the *spiritual* body of Christ (the church) should function?

The Bible contains written truth from start to finish. The first verse of the Bible tells the truth: "In the beginning God created the heavens and the earth" (Genesis 1:1). The last verse of the Bible tells the truth: "The grace of the Lord Jesus be with God's people. Amen" (Revelation 22:21). Everything in between tells the truth: "All Scripture is God-breathed" (2 Timothy 3:16). The Bible is not myths, legends, fairy tales, and pie-in-the-sky foolishness. The truth is written.

### Truth is revealed in Jesus

At Jesus' trial Pilate asked, "What is truth?" (John 18:38). All he had to do was look more closely at the one standing quietly in front of him. Several years ago *Life* magazine's Christmas issue featured a picture of Jesus on the cover, with the big question, "Who was he?" An article inside quoted a variety of views. Some said Jesus never existed. Others saw him as a well-meaning but misguided teacher, a radical feminist, or a tragic victim of circumstances. But actually the magazine's name on the cover answered its own question. Who is Jesus? Life!

Jesus doesn't need to be reinvented, reinterpreted, or reimagined. He revealed himself as Savior and Lord. He should be received as Savior and respected as Lord.

### Truth sets us free

We are free to choose whether we will *do* right or wrong, but we are not free to decide what *is* right or wrong. God decides that. We find true freedom when we live in harmony with reality as the Creator designed it.

Jesus' original listeners didn't understand what he meant when he said, "The truth will set you free." They began arguing with him, saying, "We are Abraham's descendants and have never been slaves of anyone" (John 8:31-33). But freedom stealers like the Pharisees didn't understand spiritual liberty. They used their version of truth to enslave people, loading heavy burdens on people's shoulders.

The truth will set us free. But notice, Jesus put an important condition on this promise: "If you hold to my teaching."

- When we hold to Jesus' teaching about grace and forgiveness, he can set us free from a guilty conscience and free from bitterness against others.
- When we hold to his teaching about his own lordship, we're free from trying to live up to everyone else's expectations.
- When we imitate the way he treated Samaritans and centurions, we can be free from racism and prejudice that keep people at arm's length.

- When we heed his teaching about moral purity, we'll find freedom from sexual diseases and addictions that weaken bodies, poison minds, and ruin families.
- When we take to heart his prayer for unity, we'll be set free from sectarianism that divides and distracts the church.
- When we live by the power of the Holy Spirit, he will free us from trying to live by human strength alone.

## Tolerance and Truth: Let's Get Them Together

When I conducted my truth survey, the most common response by far was, "It's hard to tell the truth when it will hurt someone's feelings." And let's face it—some of Jesus' teachings sound remarkably unpopular today:

- We are sinners.
- Hell is real.
- We're accountable to God.
- Jesus is the only way to salvation.

Truths like those can be painful to hear and painful to say. Can we find a healthy way to embrace both tolerance and truth? Jesus did. The Bible says he was "full of grace and truth" (John 1:14).

Grace isn't just a mushy feel-good-ism, and truth isn't a ball and chain. Truth is the hand God uses to guide us; grace is the hand he uses to pick us up when we fall. Truth is the Good Shepherd's rod of correction; grace is the green pasture where he makes us lie down.

"The message of the cross [*Jesus' death, burial, and resurrection*] is foolishness to those who are perishing," wrote the apostle Paul (1 Corinthians 1:18). Many people today find it offensive if we talk about sin and salvation on God's terms. We can't change the truth about the cross, even if some do find it offensive. But we need to make sure the offense doesn't come from our own attitude. If people hear our message and turn away, we need to make sure they do so because of the offense of the cross, not merely because we were rude or overbearing, or that we refused to listen to them and love them. The truth does hurt; but let's not infect the wound with a poisonous attitude.

> A remark generally hurts in proportion to its truth.[19]
>
> Will Rogers

After graduating from Bible college, Brian Fox became a youth minister, but he sensed the Lord leading him to change careers and become a lawyer.[20] He says:

> When I began law school, I was nervous that my background in ministry would hinder me in developing good friendships with my classmates. Because of that, I avoided introducing myself as "Brian Fox—former minister who still believes that Jesus is the way, the truth, and the life and that no one comes to the Father except through Jesus." Instead, I was careful to build sturdy relationships before I revealed the entirety of my background and corresponding worldview.
>
> This proved to be pretty cool. I can't tell you how many times my friends were stunned once I shared what I did before beginning law school. I was eating lunch one afternoon with a friend who'd finally started connecting the dots. Once he discovered that I didn't begin law school right after undergrad, he asked what I'd done in the interim.
>
> I told him. And then . . . silence.
>
> I broke the silence by saying something like, "You're thinking of all the terrible stories and sins you've confessed, aren't you?"

We both laughed, and then I attempted to change his mind about the notion that Christians promote judgment before grace."

Could it be that the current infatuation with tolerance in our society is really an expression of our longing for God's grace? We long to be accepted (by God and by others) in spite of our imperfections.

The good news is, God *does* offer sufficient grace—unfathomable grace, grace greater than all our sins. But he does so in harmony with his truth, not at the expense of it. Jesus was criticized for being the friend of tax collectors and sinners. He's amazingly merciful, loving, and compassionate. But Jesus doesn't say, "Go, it isn't sin anymore"; he says, "Go, and sin no more" (John 8:11, *KJV*). He doesn't just tolerate us; because he loves us, he tells us the truth about who we are and what we have done. Then if we're willing to accept it, he forgives us, washes us, saves us, and fills us with hope.

All this is possible because Christ did far more than merely tolerate wrong; he endured the penalty of Hell for us when he died on the cross for our sins.

Christians don't share our faith because of some arrogant desire to make others accept our point of view. We're persuaded that God is real and his amazing grace is a gift available to all who will receive it. When this truth becomes a fire in our bones, a light in our eyes, a path for our feet, a treasure in our hearts, and a consistent message others hear from our lips and see in our lives, then our faith will be contagious.

The truth will set us free.

And who couldn't tolerate a little more freedom?

# Honest Questions for Personal Reflection

1. Are you personally walking on the "narrow road" that leads to life (Matthew 7:14)? How do you know?

2. Refer back to the sections on relativism, pluralism, and universalism (p. 145). What have you heard from friends or in the media that would cause you to agree that these are "three troublesome trends"?

# Honest Questions for Group Discussion

## Relate

1. Which of the following do you find hard to tolerate?

\_\_\_\_ a sports fan who cheers for a team you can't stand

\_\_\_\_ a speaker or writer who uses bad grammar

\_\_\_\_ someone who acts snobbish and holier-than-thou

\_\_\_\_ conversationalists who talk endlessly about their grandchildren, their travels, their hobbies, their illnesses, or their political opinions

2. Cite from current news stories some "symptoms" that indicate that the concept of truth has lost its force in our culture.

## Reflect

3. Read Jeremiah 2:13. Jeremiah 2 identifies some "broken cisterns" the people had "dug" in a vain attempt to satisfy their spiritual thirst apart from God. Can you name any broken cisterns you've been tempted to dig in your own life? How has God been "the spring of living water" for you?

4. Christianity is both "wide" and "narrow." Note and discuss how from the following Scriptures.

| WIDE | NARROW |
|---|---|
| John 3:16 | John 14:6; Acts 4:12 |
| 1 Timothy 2:4 | 1 Timothy 2:5 |
| 2 Peter 3:9 | Acts 2:38 |
| 1 John 2:2 | 1 John 2:23 |

5. Is it possible to consistently combine tolerance and truth in our relationships with others? Name some people in public life (government leaders, TV/movie characters, athletes, coaches, teachers, comedians) who relate to others harshly. Then name others who tell the truth straightforwardly but without being harsh or judgmental.

## Respond

6. As your group concludes its study of *Honest Questions, Honest Answers*, talk about how it will affect the way you "give an answer to everyone who asks you to give the reason for the hope that you have" (1 Peter 3:15). What have you learned about how to engage in compelling conversations about your Christian faith?

7. Each group member who is willing can name a specific step or two they will take in order to help others step closer to the Lord. Then, as a group, pray for God to help you speak the truth in love (Ephesians 4:15) as you share your faith with others in the days ahead.

## Resources for Further Study

*Culture Shift: Communicating God's Truth to Our Changing World* by David W. Henderson (Grand Rapids, MI: Baker Books, 1998)

*The Closing of the American Mind: How Higher Education Has Failed Democracy and Impoverished the Souls of Today's Students* by Allan Bloom (New York: Simon & Schuster, 1987)

*The New Absolutes: How They Are Being Imposed on Us, How They Are Eroding Our Moral Landscape* by William D. Watkins (Minneapolis, MN: Bethany House, 1996)

*The New Tolerance: How a Cultural Movement Threatens to Destroy You, Your Faith, and Your Children* by Josh McDowell and Bob Hostetler (Wheaton, IL: Tyndale House, 1998)

*"True for You, But Not for Me": Deflating the Slogans That Leave Christians Speechless* by Paul Copan (Minneapolis, MN: Bethany House Publishers, 1998)

*Truth Is Stranger Than It Used to Be: Biblical Faith in a Postmodern Age* by J. Richard Middleton and Brian J. Walsh (Downers Grove, IL: InterVarsity Press, 1995)

# Clearing Up Some Misconceptions About Faith

The English words *faith* and *belief* can carry mixed messages. If my wife and I invite you to dinner and you say, "I'll definitely be there," we'd better clean the house and put some food in the oven. But if you say, "I *believe* I can come," we're uncertain. Should we "have *faith*" that you'll show up, or not?

Many who reject Christ and the church do so not because strong evidence compels them to disbelieve, but because they hold misguided ideas about what it means to believe, to have faith. Let's examine some common misconceptions.

## A. Faith is illogical—a blind leap in the dark

Many today assume that faith is completely irrational, with no basis in fact. This isn't a new idea. Tertullian, one of the early church fathers (who died about AD 200), argued that faith and reason are incompatible. "What has Athens to do with Jerusalem?" he asked. In other words, why try to blend human reason with faith in God?[1] And twentieth-century writer H. L. Mencken said, "Faith may be defined briefly as an illogical belief in the occurrence of the improbable."[2]

Over the years I have collected random comments that reveal an unbiblical, inaccurate understanding of faith—and that portray religious faith in a negative, condescending manner. Here are some examples:

- "Faith is the quality which allows us to believe what we know to be ridiculous" (from the comics page of a New York newspaper).
- Faith is "willful belief in the absence of evidence."
- "Science arises from the intellect, and religion arises from emotion" (from a newspaper advice columnist).
- "I think, therefore I don't believe" (from a university professor who leads a support group for skeptics).
- "The longer I walked down the path of reason and logic, the more beliefs I discarded" (from a former Christian who now describes himself as a secular humanist).

Those definitions differ greatly from the way the Bible talks about faith. The Lord doesn't ask us to be gullible (and believe *anything*), nor should we be cynical (and believe *nothing*). Proverbs 14:15 warns, "A simple man believes anything, but a prudent man gives thought to his steps." The right balance is to "test everything" and "hold on to the good" (1 Thessalonians 5:21), because "the heart cannot delight in what the mind rejects as false."[3]

Nowhere does the Bible define *faith* as an irrational, absurd leap in the dark. Mindless Christianity is not biblical Christianity.

The foundational rule of the Old Testament stated, "Love the LORD your God with all your heart and with all your soul and with all your strength" (Deuteronomy 6:5). God deserves a wholehearted allegiance that includes every part of our inner selves. Jesus called this commandment "the most important" precept in God's law—but he also dared to add words. Jesus said to love God "with all your mind" (Mark 12:30)—even though "mind" doesn't appear in the Old Testament version of this law. Rather than telling us to disengage our intellects, Jesus highlighted the importance of loving God thoughtfully, with our minds fully engaged.

Oswald Chambers said, "Always make it a practice to stir your own mind thoroughly to think through what you have easily believed. Your position is not really yours until you make it yours through suffering and study. The author or speaker from whom you learn the most is not the one who teaches you something you didn't know before, but the one who helps you take a truth with which you have quietly struggled, give it expression, and speak it clearly and boldly."[4]

Christian faith is not illogical; it means accepting the testimony of the biblical witnesses who accurately recorded what they saw and heard. "Faith is not believing what you know to be absurd. It is trusting what on excellent testimony appears to be true."[5] For example, John's Gospel was written so that those who read it will find evidence that persuades them to believe in Jesus (John 20:30, 31).

Let's divide beliefs into four categories[6]:

1. *Credulous beliefs* are supported by little or no evidence. Only gullible people would accept them. For example, "John F. Kennedy is still alive."

2. *Shallow beliefs* are based on weak evidence and influenced heavily by one's own personal desires or wishes. For example, "My favorite team, the Cincinnati Reds, will win the World Series this year."

3. *Mistaken beliefs* are those in which we simply get the facts wrong. I used to believe Venezuela was on the southwest side of South America—until I went there and discovered it's actually located on the northern-most coast of the continent.

4. *Substantive beliefs,* however, are undergirded by solid evidence so strong, it's unlikely you would ever change your mind about them. Without any fear of contradiction, I believe the Cincinnati Reds won the World Series in 1990. I also believe that a real, historical figure named Saul of Tarsus persecuted Christians in the first century, then was converted into a committed believer who traveled the world as a missionary for the faith he previously opposed.

When Christians talk about faith, we're not arguing for credulous, shallow, or mistaken beliefs. Our convictions are substantive beliefs, supported by a wide range of credible evidence.

Faith requires assent—a mental willingness to affirm or agree with a fact, based on the sufficiency of the evidence. Even if you have never been to Hawaii, you believe its climate is warm and pleasant. Even if you have never been to the Arctic Circle, you're quite sure it's cold there. Other credible witnesses have visited those places, so you trust their testimony. Likewise, it's reasonable to affirm that Jesus rose from the dead, because of the credible testimony of those who saw the risen Lord (1 Corinthians 15:3-8). And though we have not seen God with our own eyes, it's reasonable to believe that he exists—for many reasons, starting with what we can see in creation (see Psalm 19:1, 2; Romans 1:19, 20).

Faith also involves trust—a decision of the will—a voluntary choice to place oneself or one's property into the hands of a trustworthy person. You exercise trust when you pay a mechanic to fix your car, leave your children with a babysitter, fly in a plane, or allow a barber to change your appearance with a few swift snips of the scissors.

*Saving* faith involves more than mere intellectual assent or lip service to God's existence. Even the demons believe that God exists, but they tremble in the face of coming judgment (James 2:19) because they have never trusted God enough to surrender their will to him.

Jack Cottrell sums it up this way:

- prerequisite of faith: understanding
- faith per se: assent (believing *that*) and trust (believing *in* or *on*)
- result of faith: obedience[7]

Trust is the part of faith that looks irrational to an unbeliever. If you don't know my wife, you might not understand why I trust her not to overspend when she goes shopping with our credit card. Likewise, if you don't know the Lord, you may not understand why Christians tithe, pray, give, and trust God even when our circumstances seem to contradict God's wisdom and goodness.

Properly understood, faith isn't irrational or illogical. It's a reasonable alternative to unbelief. Faith isn't leaping blindly into the dark; it's leaping confidently into the light. True faith makes us "sure of what we hope for and certain of what we do not see" (Hebrews 11:1).

## B. In religious beliefs, sincerity is all that matters

Another popular misconception is that sincerity alone determines the validity of one's faith. Some insist, "It doesn't matter what you believe as long as you're sincere."

Of course, we should be sincere about our faith. Jesus reserved some of his harshest words for hypocrites who devalued the truth by their insincerity and phoniness. But sincerity isn't the only issue.

No matter how sincerely I believe that my Honda Civic will win the Indianapolis 500, I'm mistaken. No matter how earnestly I think that I could jump from the top of the Empire State Building without harming myself, I'll die if I attempt it. Would you submit to surgery under the shaky hands of a surgeon who sincerely cares about her patients ("she means well") but lacks the skill to operate successfully? If you work as a chef in a restaurant, would you keep your job very long if you sincerely care about your customers but the food tastes terrible?

In biblical times, the Jews were "zealous for God," but their zeal was "not based on knowledge" (Romans 10:2). They were sincere but wrong. Before Saul of Tarsus became a Christian, he opposed Christianity so earnestly that he persecuted the church and tried to destroy it (Galatians 1:13); later he admitted that he had been acting "in ignorance and unbelief" (1 Timothy 1:13). He was sincere but wrong.

Sincerity is important, but it isn't the only thing that matters.

## C. Faith is completely subjective and relative—what's true for you isn't necessarily true for someone else

Subjective feelings refer to perceptions of reality as experienced by the individual—the *inside-of-me* feelings, preferences, and interpretations that vary from one person to another.

Objective facts, on the other hand, refer to realities that exist independent of any reflections or feelings—the *outside-of-me* kind of truth that others can perceive and verify regardless of personal biases.

Subjectively, my wife doesn't like football the way I do, but she agrees to the objective reality that a football field is one hundred yards long. I don't enjoy shopping in craft stores the way she does, but objectively, I can show that the items there are overpriced. (Oops, my subjective biases are showing!)

Candy and I were married on August 31, 1975. You could verify that objective fact by viewing a marriage license on file in a government office in Bay Shore, New York. You could interview guests who attended the ceremony. Our wedding photos, the wedding rings we wear, the three children we have raised together, and even our joint income tax returns all bear objective testimony to the reality that Candy and I are husband and wife.

Subjectively, I have many feelings for Candy. I like the way she looks, the way she cooks, and the way she tolerates the time I spend writing books! Our marriage thrives when we express romantic love toward one another. But even on those days when we don't feel so great about each other—and let's be honest, every married couple does have those days!—nothing can change the objective truth that we stood before witnesses on August 31, 1975, and committed ourselves to be husband and wife.

Likewise, Christian faith involves both objective facts and subjective feelings. Jesus Christ lived in real history. An article in *U.S. News & World Report* stated:

The fact that Jesus . . . was executed in Roman-occupied Palestine is one part of the Passion story that modern historians believe is well corroborated by extra-Biblical sources. The Roman historian Tacitus, for example, writing in A.D. 110 of the persecution of Christians under the emperor Nero, refers to followers of "Christ, whom the procurator Pontius Pilate had executed in the reign of Tiberius." . . .

Striking corroboration of the type of crucifixion that is described in the Gospels was discovered in 1968 at an excavation site near Mount Scopus, just northeast of Jerusalem. Three tombs were found at the site, one of them containing the remains of a man who had been crucified between A.D. 7 and 70. The man's feet had been nailed together at the heels, his forearms had nail wounds and the bones of his lower legs had been broken—wounds that are entirely consistent with the description in John's Gospel of the crucifixion of Jesus and the two thieves.[8]

Jesus died on a wooden cross so real you could have gotten a splinter from it. He rose from the dead, leaving behind an empty tomb and neatly folded grave clothes examined by eyewitnesses (John 20:1-9). A slab of stone was found in Nazareth, the childhood home of Jesus, by archaeologists in 1878. It contains an inscription known as the Nazareth Decree issued by the Roman emperor Claudius, who ruled from AD 41 to 54. The emperor decreed that no graves should be disturbed or bodies removed from them, and anyone violating the rule would "be sentenced to capital punishment on the charge of violation of sepulcher," which seems like a pretty harsh punishment for disturbing graves. Norman Geisler observes, "A likely explanation is that Claudius, having heard of the Christian doctrine of Resurrection . . . decided not to let any such report surface again. . . . This is early testimony to the strong and persistent belief that Jesus rose from the dead."[9]

These biblical events really happened. They are objective realities, regardless of how anyone feels about them. We worship a God who is really there, who exists regardless of how we feel about him.

Now, our subjective reactions to all this may vary. As a Christian, I feel a deep sense of gratitude to God for what he's done for me. I want to honor, worship, and obey him because I've learned to trust him. My relationship with Christ is personal and precious to me, and sometimes during moments of quiet reflection or corporate worship, I find myself almost overwhelmed by love for the Son of God who died for me. But my faith is not based simply on what I feel in my heart. It's rooted in objective facts and historical realities.

## D. It's fine to talk about faith at church, but not in the public arena

On the contrary, God calls us to *live* by faith, not to see faith as one small compartment of life. People aren't bookstores with different sections marked "Health," "Social Life," "Work," "Family," "Finances," and "Religion." Faith should affect everything we do, naturally finding its way into our conversations in a variety of settings.

Ravi Zacharias points out three levels on which philosophical dialogue occurs:

1. theory (or logic)
2. the arts (media)
3. table-talk (ordinary conversation that happens around the kitchen table, in restaurants, and dorm rooms)

Zacharias says, "Argue at level one, illustrate at level two, and apply at level three."[10]

In the New Testament, believers answered questions and talked about their faith in a wide variety of settings:

- at open-air gatherings (Acts 2:14-41)
- on the road (8:26-39)
- in houses of worship (13:14-48)
- at riverside meeting sites (16:13-15)
- in prisons (16:22-34)
- in shopping malls or marketplaces (17:16-21)
- in government hearing rooms (17:22-31; 25:1–26:32)
- in private homes (18:26; 20:20)
- in lecture halls (19:9)
- aboard ships (27:1-26)

## E. Faith is impractical and boring—it's for supersaints and religious geeks who are into that sort of thing

"So you're involved in church? Good for you," some folks say with a nod, but also with a look on their faces that says they're personally not interested. "It's fine if you're into that kind of thing," they say, while edging away from the conversation, as if going to church sounds like one of the most boring activities they could ever imagine.

But wait a minute. Faith isn't just for supersaints. Everyone lives by faith in something or someone.

All history is based on faith. We haven't met George Washington, Christopher Columbus, or Alexander the Great in person, but we believe they existed because we know certain things they did and said.

Daily life requires faith. If you eat in a restaurant, you trust a cook you probably will never see—and depend on him not to poison your food. If you fly in an airplane, you place your life in the hands of the pilot—and trust in the overwhelming probability that he is sober and properly trained.

Everyone exercises faith. The question is, "Who (or What) is the *object* of your faith?" If you don't believe in the Lord, that doesn't mean you have no faith; it means you are placing your faith somewhere else.

Where do people get the idea that serious faith is mainly for religious geeks? To be honest, some Christians *are* boring, as are some worship services, sermons, and Bible classes. But so are lots of other experiences in life that most people consider meaningful and necessary, like going to school, paying bills, and washing dishes. Christians don't have a corner on boredom. Everyone has to deal with day-to-day realities at work, school, or in your personal life that seem dull and routine. Plus, boredom isn't a good test of truth. (Brushing your teeth is boring, but it's essential for your health.)

Countless Christians live incredibly adventurous and interesting lives, but unfortunately, some folks carry around the false impression that serving God is dull.

A single professional named Cathy told me, "The way I look at it, people who go to church live squeaky-clean lives, and I don't. I live a fast life, and they don't. They don't have fun, and they don't know what is out in the world. They live in closed, protected environments. They kind of go off by themselves. They are cloistered people, with no sense of reality."

Her description sounds a lot different from the believers we encounter in Scripture. Simon Peter was brash, rough-cut, and fast-talking. "Squeaky-clean"? I don't think so. First-century Christians in big cities like Corinth or Ephesus were surrounded by sexual immorality, occult religions, and pagan philosophies every time they ventured into the marketplace. "Cloistered"? Hardly.

The apostle Paul's travels sound like a modern adventurer's itinerary: Athens, Jerusalem, Cyprus, Rome . . . He was beaten, stoned, shipwrecked, and endangered by everything from bandits to false teachers. He endured so much that he often went without sleep, and he knew how it felt to be hungry, thirsty, cold, and naked (2 Corinthians 11:24-27). A "closed, protected environment"? No way.

At the same time, Paul experienced such a deep sense of purpose and fulfillment that his letters overflow with joy and peace (Philippians 4:4-7, for example).

Christians don't choose a safe, bland, easy way of life. It takes guts to follow the road less traveled and commit ourselves to Jesus' kind of humble service and self-discipline. And yet, like Jesus himself who endured the cross "for the joy set before him" (Hebrews 12:2), Christians have fun, laugh at life's absurdities, and enjoy good humor—all with the added delight of sensing that somehow the God of grace is chuckling along with us!

All things considered, the life of an all-out, sold-out, Spirit-filled, service-minded Christ follower is anything but dull.

So here's faith as the Bible describes it:

- Faith comes by hearing God's Word (Romans 10:17; 1 Peter 1:25).
- Faith means trusting in God's promises even when we can't see tangible proof (John 20:29; 2 Corinthians 4:18; Hebrews 11:1-3, 27; 1 Peter 1:8). But it's grounded in the testimony of credible eyewitnesses who *did* see tangible proof (John 20:30, 31; 2 Peter 1:16).
- Faith is an active expression of reliance on God, not merely a passive state. "Faith without deeds is dead" (James 2:24-26). Faith is supposed to be a way of life. We "live by faith" (2 Corinthians 5:7; Galatians 3:11; also see Hebrews 11).
- Faith in God leads to obedience. If we call Jesus our Lord, we'll want to do what he says (Luke 6:46; John 14:15; Romans 1:5; 16:26).
- Faith stabilizes us in difficult times. "It is by faith you stand firm" (2 Corinthians 1:24; see also 1 Peter 1:6-9; Revelation 14:12).
- Faith is forward looking. It doesn't demand immediate results, but looks ahead to the ultimate realization of God's promises (2 Corinthians 4:13, 14).
- Faith is an indispensable ingredient in our relationship with God. "Without faith it is impossible to please God" (Hebrews 11:6).

- "The faith," in the Bible, sometimes means a clear, discernible body of biblical beliefs or teachings. Jude says to "contend for the faith that was once for all entrusted to the saints" (Jude 3). Paul says there is "one Lord, one faith, one baptism" (Ephesians 4:5). He devoted his life to the task of keeping and spreading "the faith" (1 Timothy 4:1-6; 2 Timothy 4:7).

- Faith is more powerful than many people realize. "This is the victory that has overcome the world, even our faith" (1 John 5:4).

# More Questions and Answers

## A. Bible—What kind of book is it?

As noted in chapter 2, the word *Bible* comes from the Greek *biblos,* which means a "book" (or "scroll"). *Biblos* is the first word in the Greek New Testament, for Matthew 1:1 refers to the "record [*or book*] of the genealogy of Jesus Christ." The word also refers to the "book of Moses" (Mark 12:26), the "book of the words of Isaiah" (Luke 3:4), and even the occult books used by the sorcerers in Ephesus (Acts 19:19). John used a similar word, *biblion* ("little book"), when he observed that Jesus performed many more miraculous signs than John's Gospel could contain (John 20:30), and Paul used it when he asked Timothy to bring him his scrolls—small, personal copies of portions of the Scripture (2 Timothy 4:13).[1]

Total books in the Old Testament: thirty-nine, originally written in Hebrew (with small portions in Aramaic, a dialect of Hebrew). Total books in the New Testament: twenty-seven, originally written in Greek.

The Bible was the first major book ever printed (by Johannes Gutenberg in 1456).[2] There are now more than 450 complete Bible translations. And portions of the Bible have been translated into more than 2,500 of the world's 6,500 languages and dialects—far more than any other book.[3] The Bible has even made it to the moon—taken there by the Apollo 14 moon mission in 1971.[4]

The Bible possesses an amazing internal harmony despite the

diversity of its authorship. It's actually a library of sixty-six books, written over a period of approximately 1,500 years by thirty to forty different authors. It contains historical narratives, poetic songs, personal letters, fascinating character studies, short stories, parables, witty proverbs, mind-boggling visions, and frank descriptions of real people who often failed more than they succeeded. Yet despite their varied literary styles and personalities, the writers focused on one key theme (God's unfolding plan of redemption) and dealt with controversial issues without contradicting themselves.

## B. Evangelism—Why do Christians try to push their ideas onto others?

Dick Alexander, senior minister with LifeSpring Christian Church in Cincinnati, Ohio, described an encounter he had with a Jewish friend who worked with him in a community organization for a number of years.[5] "Levi [*not his real name*] was a community leader, well known and respected," Dick said. "We served in a number of projects together. I liked him, and sometimes prayed for him."

One day at lunch Dick decided to raise the issue of Jesus. Smiling, Levi responded, "Are you trying to convert me?"

"The directness of his reply caught me off guard," Dick remembers. "I thought my initiation of spiritual conversation had been thoughtful and not pushy. I didn't have a quick, witty reply. But I didn't deny that in my care for him I hoped he would consider Jesus. Unfortunately, his reply was a conversation stopper."

Dick says, "I've replayed that lunch many times, wondering if there might have been a different way—some other entry point that would have opened the door."

In a culture that resists pushy attempts to "convert" anyone, how do we explain why Christians desire to lead others to Christ?

*Rightly understood, evangelism is a loving act.* Christians shouldn't try to win arguments for arguments' sake or try to demonstrate spiritual superiority. "Christ's love compels us" (2 Corinthians 5:14) to point others to the Lord, the source of eternal hope.

*Evangelism requires hearing as well as telling.* Believers should listen carefully to the questions our friends are asking. Often their stories will open doors for us to share the gospel.

*Evangelism means persuasion, not arm twisting.* We can be bold about our faith without being obnoxious. Our goal isn't to push our ideas onto others, but like the apostle Paul, we're also "not ashamed of the gospel" (Romans 1:16). Paul "proved," "explained," and gave evidence that Jesus was the Christ (Acts 9:22; 17:3). He often "reasoned" with others about the gospel (Acts 17:2, 3, 17; 18:4, 19). He considered himself ready to "defend" or "confirm" the gospel (Philippians 1:7, 16). When people believed his message, they were "persuaded" (Acts 17:4; 18:4; 19:8).

## C. Evangelism—Does one size fit all?

While the core of our *message* must always remain the same, we should adapt our *methods* of sharing the gospel to fit the background and needs of others. The apostle Paul described his approach in 1 Corinthians 9:19-22: "Though I am free and belong to no man, I make myself a slave to everyone, to win as many as possible. To the Jews I became like a Jew, to win the Jews. . . . To those not having the law [*the Gentiles*] I became like one not having the law. . . . I have become all things to all men so that by all possible means I might save some."

What was Paul saying? Was he advocating a wishy-washy compromise of God's truth? That we become spiritual chameleons who simply adopt the standards of our changing culture and blend with the world around us? No! Paul hastens to add: "I do all this for the sake of the gospel, that I may share in its blessings" (v. 23). Paul never advocated anything less than the complete and accurate gospel message. But he was willing to adapt the *method* of its presentation because he was determined to communicate the message with maximum effectiveness in every culture. Although he was free in Christ, he was willing to walk in the shoes of others—to understand their worldview and present the gospel in words they could understand.

There were profound differences between Jews (those "with the law") and Gentiles (those "without the law"). The Jews were familiar with the Hebrew Scriptures, which they had learned from childhood and their rabbis had taught for generations. They were monotheists who believed in the one true God. Since they were familiar with the messianic prophecies written by Isaiah, Jeremiah, Daniel, and other prophets of God, they eagerly anticipated the Messiah's coming. They were familiar with the Spirit and power of God, as well as the miracles performed through the ministries of Spirit-filled men like Moses and Elijah. Thus, Paul says, "Jews demand miraculous signs."

The Gentiles, on the other hand, were unfamiliar with the Scriptures. They didn't know Adam from Amos. They were polytheists (they believed in many gods). They knew little or nothing about messianic prophecies or a future intervention by a coming Savior. The Gentiles were familiar with philosophical approaches to God. Thus, Paul says, "Greeks look for wisdom" (1 Corinthians 1:22).

Many religious seekers today fit into one of those two categories. Some, like the first-century Jews, are familiar with the Bible but not satisfied with it. Preoccupied with spiritual gifts and special powers, they "demand miraculous signs" and, before they will believe, want personal verification that God exists. Others, like the first-century Gentiles, know little about the Bible but "look for wisdom"—that is, they're constantly searching for a new system of thought that will explain everything according to human logic and reasoning.

To both groups Paul said, "We preach Christ crucified: a stumbling block to Jews and foolishness to Gentiles" (v. 23). And the gospel had its effect. Thousands of Jews and Gentiles gladly embraced it and discovered that Christ is indeed "the power of God and the wisdom of God. For the foolishness of God is wiser than man's wisdom, and the weakness of God is stronger than man's strength" (vv. 24, 25).

What does all this have to do with reaching postmodern people? Three points:

*1. It's vital to find common ground with seekers.* This does not mean we compromise with evil or betray our Christian values. It simply means establishing a point of contact, a place of common understanding. There will be some points you and your non-Christian friend can agree on as a starting point for discussion—a landing strip where you can come down with the gospel.

*2. A key issue is the position of the non-Christian with regard to the Bible.* Even some who don't have an active faith in Christ at least have a positive orientation toward God and a certain degree of respect for the Bible. Perhaps a kind relative quoted Scripture and took them to Sunday school when they were children. With friends like these, we can go directly to the Scriptures to show God's plan of salvation and his will for our lives. But in a postmodern culture characterized by a growing ignorance of the Bible and foggy ideas about God, and in which fewer children have been brought up attending Sunday school, we have to do more foundational work. Before presenting the plan of salvation, we may need to teach Monotheism 101 and answer questions like these:

- "Who is God?"
- "Why should we believe the Bible is God's Word?"
- "What is the basic message of the Bible?"
- "What makes the Bible different from other books?"

Today we can't assume our friends know and believe the foundational truths familiar to most Christians. Increasingly, our culture is becoming more "Gentile" than "Jewish," more like Athens than Jerusalem.

*3. No matter the audience, we must present the facts of Jesus' death, burial, and resurrection—the very core of the gospel.* Whether the apostles spoke to Jews or Gentiles, they emphasized the death and resurrection of Christ and invited their listeners to respond to the good news. Jesus' cross and empty tomb will never lose relevance. Although the starting points may differ as we encounter different people and their questions, our goal must be the same with everyone: to introduce them to Christ and his life-changing power. In every culture the gospel is still the power of God for salvation (Romans 1:16).

## D. Evil—Why do Christians blame evil on the devil?

Here's how I once heard the question:

*If God created everything, why did he create Satan? And if he's all-powerful, why doesn't he just nuke Satan and get it over with? For myself this is a rhetorical question, since I don't believe in Satan (mostly just in human stupidity, which usually looks identical), but I'd still like your take on it. My view from the peanut gallery: To blame all this world's bad stuff on a devil externalizes our own dark side and removes our personal responsibility for those nasty actions. "The devil made me do it" is no excuse.*

My response:

You're right that "The devil made me do it" is no excuse. We're personally responsible for our actions. But the Bible portrays Satan as a real personality. (For example, Jesus conversed with him—see Matthew 4:1-11.) The devil is a formidable enemy of God's people, but his spiritual power is not equivalent to God's (Ephesians 6:10-13; James 4:7; 1 Peter 5:8, 9; 1 John 4:4). Based on his track record described in the Bible, it's clear that Satan tempts people to sin, twists the truth (Genesis 3:1-6), and even pretends to be "an angel of light" (2 Corinthians 11:14).

To be honest, assigning "all this world's bad stuff" to mere "human stupidity" strikes me as naive. There's a ton of genuine evil out there. The Holocaust and the 9/11 terrorist attacks aren't just stupid acts; they are evil acts. So are child abuse and cruelty of all kinds. Evil is real; it's deadly. It's the opposite of the healthy life God wants for us. *Evil* is *live* spelled backwards!

Why did God create Satan? For the same reason, I suppose, that all other free-will beings (angelic and human) were created: to experience the joy that comes from serving and worshipping God. But instead of serving God, Satan rebelled and became (by his own choice, apparently) God's adversary who twists the truth and tries to lead others astray (see John 8:44; 2 Peter 2:4; Jude 6; Revelation 12:9; 20:1-3, 7, 8).

Why doesn't God "just nuke Satan and get it over with"? It's only a matter of time. Jesus came the first time "to destroy the devil's work" (1 John 3:8) and "destroy him who holds the power of death—that is, the devil" (Hebrews 2:14). When Jesus comes back the next time, it'll be all over for Satan—and "nuking" is a pretty accurate way to describe what will happen to him (see Revelation 20:10).

## E. God—Isn't God just a crutch for the weak?

Some non-Christians hint, with a bit of condescension, "Isn't faith in God (or the idea of God) just a crutch, a comforting intoxicant for those too weak to face life on their own? If you're strong, hard-working, and self-sufficient, why do you need to lean on God? Shouldn't you just take responsibility for your own life instead of depending on God to comfort you and take care of you?"

Others have the impression that believers are somehow out of touch with the real world. "It's fine for you to believe in God and go to church if you feel the need for something like that," they say. "But I don't." (To a Christian, it sounds strange when someone says, "I don't feel the need for God"—a bit like saying, "Well, it's fine if you feel like you need to breathe air. But me? I don't need air to survive!")

As psychiatrist Sigmund Freud (1856–1939) analyzed the religious beliefs of his patients, he came to an interesting conclusion that he described in a short book, *The Future of an Illusion.* Freud argued that instead of men and women being created in the image of God, it's really the other way around; we created God by wishing for a divine Father figure, a protector to help us when we're afraid.[6]

If Freud was right, then faith in God is little more than wishful thinking, a product of human weakness and fear. This view implies that as we become more mature, we should grow out of our childish dependence on God and learn to face life bravely on our own.

Karl Marx (1818–1883) added his own twist. Religion, he insisted, is "the opiate of the masses"[7]—a way to keep ordinary people pacified in drug-like contentment while the rich and powerful exploit them.

According to the skeptic Bertrand Russell, "Religion is based, I think, primarily and mainly upon fear. It is partly the terror of the unknown and partly . . . the wish to feel that you have a kind of elder brother who will stand by you in all your troubles and disputes. Fear is the basis of the whole thing—fear of the mysterious, fear of defeat, fear of death."[8]

Years ago a cereal commercial said, "Trix are for kids." Today many people assume that *faith* is for kids; out in the real world, you'd better put away childish things and fend for yourself.

But if faith is based on fear, ignorance, and immaturity, then how do you explain the fact that people of great learning, courage, and maturity believe strongly in God?

Christians freely admit our need for God. Doesn't it make sense that the created would desire fellowship with the Creator? Is it a surprise when a child reaches for the security of her father's arms? Isn't it logical that imperfect people would want to honor a perfect God? As someone has said, "God is not a crutch—he's a stretcher! We couldn't even limp into Heaven without him."

C. S. Lewis argued that for every need, something exists to fulfill that need.[9] Ducks feel the need to swim; there is such a thing as water. Human beings feel the need to eat; thankfully, there is such a thing as food. So if we feel the need for God, isn't it logical to think there is a God who can fulfill that need?

God *is* a crutch we can lean on. He "gives strength to the weary and increases the power of the weak" (Isaiah 40:29). He is "the Father of compassion and the God of all comfort, who comforts us in all our troubles, so that we can comfort those in any trouble with the comfort we ourselves have received from God" (2 Corinthians 1:3, 4).

Some folks think of God solely as a comforter, while others see him mainly as a threat. Some see him as a kind Father, others as a harsh judge. But the important issue is what the Bible says about God, not our preconceived ideas about him. Not only does the Bible tell us that God exists; it tells us what kind of God he is. And he is not the kind of God we would invent, even if we tried.

Ancient pagan gods? Their worshippers tried to appease and manipulate them to gain a better harvest or win an important battle. The gods of the Greeks and Romans? Those so-called deities displayed the same moral frailties common to human beings—selfishness, unrestrained anger, lust. That's what happens when people create their own gods.

But the God of the Bible is holy, all-powerful, eternal, and unchanging. It's unlikely we would invent a god like that simply to make ourselves feel better—especially since he is also a sovereign God who requires our obedience and compliance to his will. Christians voluntarily surrender to this one who is wiser and more powerful than we are, while atheism tries to "kick sand in the face of God."[10]

God is more than a comforter, more than a soft-spoken Savior who soothes our hurts. He's also our Master and Ruler, the Lord of Heaven and earth. He's a God of grace and mercy, but he's also the all-knowing presence who is always looking "through a keyhole"[11] of our lives, aware of our every thought and our every move—a God from whom there is no escape (Psalm 139:1-12). "Everything is uncovered and laid bare before the eyes of him to whom we must give account" (Hebrews 4:13). Who could invent a God like that? Who would even want to?

Christians don't create a god who makes us feel good; we accept the authority of God who rules our lives, whether we're comfortable or not. Instead of wishing God into existence, it's more reasonable to think that some people try to wish God *out* of existence because they don't want to be subject to his moral restrictions. According to Romans 1:18, people "suppress the truth by their wickedness." "God's invisible qualities—his eternal power and divine nature—have been clearly seen, being understood from what has been made, so that men are without excuse" (Romans 1:20). But sin hardens hearts and sears consciences, making it harder to believe the self-evident reality that God exists.

Jesus never told his disciples, "Lean on your crutch and follow me." He did say, "Take up your cross and follow me" (see Matthew 16:24). A cross is hardly a crutch.

Yes, many people do treat God as a crutch. But that's a reasonable thing to do, since all of us are "crippled." Even an atheist leans on something. The question is, "Which crutch will you choose—and which has more evidence to support it?" Will you lean on God, or as one seeker told me, will you just "go have another gin and tonic and play a little harder"?

## F. Heaven—What will it be like?

Here are some of my favorite descriptions of Heaven from the book of Revelation:

- More exciting than the Super Bowl—"a great multitude that no one could count, from every nation, tribe, people and language, standing before the throne and in front of the Lamb" (Revelation 7:9).
- Lasting refreshment and peace that's infinitely better than a great vacation—"They will rest from their labor, for their deeds will follow them" (14:13).
- Joyful celebration that surpasses the best party you've ever attended—"Blessed are those who are invited to the wedding supper of the Lamb!" (19:9).
- Spiritual fulfillment that satisfies our souls' deepest longings—"Now the dwelling of God is with men, and he will live with them. They will be his people, and God himself will be with them and be their God" (21:3).

- Emotional wholeness that comes from the elimination of suffering once and for all—"He will wipe every tear from their eyes. There will be no more death or mourning or crying or pain" (21:4).
- Meaningful, satisfying work—"No longer will there be any curse. . . . His servants will serve him" (22:3).

The Bible fascinates me with its portrayals of Heaven's golden streets, crystal-clear water, and brilliant light. But my favorite picture of eternity for the believer is this simple metaphor: going home. "We live by faith, not by sight. We are confident, I say, and would prefer to be away from the body and at home with the Lord" (2 Corinthians 5:7, 8).

*At home with the Lord!*

Jesus promised to go and prepare a place for us in his Father's house (John 14:1-4). It's a place where the table is always spread and the family always gets along. A place where no one is abused, rejected, or ignored. A safe place. A holy place. A place where no one ever says good-bye.

Heaven won't be a boring place with nothing to do but sit on a cloud and strum a harp. I imagine it will be more like this:

- a person who likes to build things having all the time and materials he could ever need to construct great masterpieces
- a person who likes to read and learn having time to consume every book she'd ever want to read
- a person who enjoys athletics being able to run and jump without getting tired
- a person who likes to travel having unlimited opportunities to explore the vast array of God's "new heaven and new earth"
- a person who enjoys music having unlimited opportunity to compose and perform beautiful songs of praise to God
- a person whose dreams and aspirations have been frustrated here on earth finding deep, unending fulfillment at last

- a person who has been misunderstood or belittled by others here on earth finding himself enveloped at last in God's abiding love
- a person who was blind on earth, now with wide-open eyes beholding the glorious colors and splendors of Heaven
- a person who was paralyzed on earth, now leaping with joy
- a person who was lonely now enjoying sweet, untainted fellowship with dear old saints who served the Lord for years, with little children whose lives were snuffed out prematurely, and with faithful servants of God who believed God's promises even when others around them succumbed to sin and doubt
- a person who has asked hard questions and never felt completely content with the answers he received—yet trusted God anyway—finally experiencing a satisfied mind
- and all of us who've been saved by grace, worshipping the all-wise Lord who deserves all praise

## G. Hell—Is it reasonable to believe in eternal punishment?

It would be hard to come up with a subject that makes us squirm more than this one.

Bertrand Russell wrote, "There is one very serious defect to my mind in Christ's moral character, and that is that He believed in hell. I do not myself feel that any person who is really profoundly humane can believe in everlasting punishment."[12]

But no matter how uncomfortable it makes us, we can't avoid the Bible's frank teaching about Hell. Jesus had a lot to say about it (Matthew 13:42, 50; 25:41; Mark 9:43-48; Luke 13:23-28; 16:23-28; John 5:28, 29). So did Paul (2 Thessalonians 1:6-9), Peter (2 Peter 3:7), Jude (5-7, 13-15), and John (Revelation 20:10-15). The reality of Hell motivates us to live holy lives (Matthew 10:28) and increases our appreciation for Christ, who rescued us from the punishment we deserve (Romans 5:8-10). (The Christian message of salvation loses much of its urgency if there's nothing to be saved *from*.) The worst part of Hell will be missing out on the blessings of Heaven.

Curiously enough, the New Testament, which says so much about God's gracious gift of salvation, tells us more than the Old Testament does about Hell. In addition to the plain teaching of Scripture, here are five other lines of argument that show that it's reasonable to believe in the reality of Hell.

*1. Justice requires it.* "Human experience has universally taught the concept that when you break a rule, you ought to be punished," says Johnny Pressley, dean of the graduate seminary at Cincinnati Christian University, who teaches a course on the doctrine of Hell.[13] "In every culture and every age, parents have punished their children for disobeying their authority. Societies have established laws and ways to enforce those laws. If you believe there's a Creator who has created us, and thus has authority over us, it's not unreasonable to say that this Creator has some expectations, and if we violate them, he will punish us just as we punish those who are under our authority."

Dr. Pressley continues, "The punishment for a crime is often conditioned upon the greatness of the offense. If a neighbor shoots my dog or cat, I can get legal recourse, but we would never execute someone for that. If he shoots my son or daughter, the killer will pay a greater penalty. But if he shoots the president of the United States, we call it assassination and deal with it as a much more serious matter—because the greater the person who is offended, the greater we think the penalty ought to be." When we apply this to God, we "can see how the penalty ought to increase by proportion. How high a penalty should someone pay for offending an infinite God?"

*2. God's authority as Creator harmonizes with it.* "If you build something, you can tear it down if you wish," Pressley points out. "If you paint a picture and you don't want anyone to see it, you don't have to show it to anybody. It's yours. Nobody can tell you what you can and can't do with your creation. A person may feel like, *This is the way things ought to be. God shouldn't give us rules, and if he does, he shouldn't punish or send anyone to Hell.* But it's illogical for us to say that the Creator must do what we're thinking and feeling. Rather, we should be asking God, 'What is it you want us to do?'"

*3. God's work as Redeemer underscores the reality of Hell.* "Any effort on our part to minimize the punishment of sinners will also at the same time minimize the pain of Calvary," Pressley explains. "If God never truly punishes sin, then there's no way to account for the horrible suffering Jesus endured on the cross. You can't minimize Hell without minimizing the atonement that keeps us from going there."

*4. It's not surprising that someone who has broken God's law would try to deny the reality of Hell.* "In every culture, when someone has a guilty conscience he tries to rationalize, justify, defend, and do whatever he can to get out of any guilt and any penalty. We're always hopeful that we won't get caught; then if we get caught, we hope we won't be punished. We try to get a good lawyer, and hope the jury will set us free," Pressley notes. "And when it comes to God, we hope there isn't a day of judgment, a day of accounting—so we're always open to any suggestion that will give us a way past a God who judges. Guilty, sinful people have an inherent fear of facing God as judge. The devil holds us in slavery to our fear of death (Hebrews 2:14, 15). So the devil can offer dozens of deceptions and we'll grab them."

*5. God's grace offers hope.* What about people who have never heard of Christ? "God's grace has already been broader in our lives than we would have imagined, so we don't know how far his grace will go with others," Pressley observes. "What we know is, the Scripture clearly teaches that we must be saved through Jesus Christ (Acts 4:12). We know there's a Great Commission that tells us to go to all the world—everyone needs to hear the name of Jesus. Romans 3:23 says that 'all have sinned.' So I view the world as lost, but I don't put the world in Hell. I let God the judge do so based on both his justice and his grace, trusting him to do what is appropriate. I preach more a plan of salvation than a word of condemnation."

## H. Hope—If hope is real, why does life seem so pointless?

An ancient tombstone inscription used by Roman pagans contained what evidently was meant to be a little joke about death. Translated from the Latin it means: "I was not, I am not, I care not."[14] Most of us wouldn't express our feelings of despair so blatantly, but we do comprehend how miserable it would be to live without hope.

It might surprise you to learn that the Bible contains an entire book that takes an honest look at the seeming pointlessness of life. King Solomon asked a lot of honest questions in Ecclesiastes. As someone has said, "Ecclesiastes asks the questions the rest of the Bible answers."

Solomon begins the book with a depressing observation: "Meaningless! Meaningless! . . . Utterly meaningless! Everything is meaningless" (Ecclesiastes 1:2). It's actually the Hebrew word *abel*, which other translations render as "emptiness" or "vanity." Like the man named Abel whom we meet in the book of Genesis, whose life was cut short by his angry brother Cain, *abel* means "short-lived" or "transitory," like a puff of air.[15] Life seems brief, empty, pointless. It's like chasing after the wind, trying to grasp air in your hand.

*What about education?* Solomon devoted himself to study. According to 1 Kings 4:32-34, he became a world-renowned expert on literature (he wrote three thousand proverbs), music (he composed more than one thousand songs), botany (he described a wide range of plant life), and biology (he taught about animals, birds, reptiles, and fish). But education alone isn't the key to a satisfying life. While it's good to learn all we can, in the process we're likely to discover many problems we can't solve on our own. "What is twisted cannot be straightened; what is lacking cannot be counted. . . . The more knowledge, the more grief" (Ecclesiastes 1:15, 18).

*What about pleasure?* Solomon said, "I tried cheering myself with wine, and embracing folly" (2:3). He became an expert at fooling around, making small talk, making people laugh. But even if you're the life of the party, what will you do when the party's over? A vacation, a holiday, a fun evening with friends . . . it soon ends. What then? Just surviving from one weekend to the next? Solomon experimented with all kinds of pleasure. But "that also proved to be meaningless," he eventually had to admit (2:1).

*What about possessions?* Solomon tried that route too. He built houses, vineyards, gardens, and tree-lined parks for himself. His palace took thirteen years to build, had rooms paneled with sweet-smelling cedar, and was half the length of a football field. In a day when clean water wasn't readily available, he "made reservoirs to water groves of flourishing trees" (1 Kings 7:1-12; Ecclesiastes 2:4-6). He owned servants to care for his property, vast herds to provide plenty of meat, choirs of singers to entertain him, a "bank account" overflowing with silver and gold, and plenty of women to meet his sexual desires (Ecclesiastes 2:7-9). "I denied myself nothing my eyes desired; I refused my heart no pleasure," he said (v. 10). But all the things money could buy still left him saying that "everything was meaningless, a chasing after the wind; nothing was gained under the sun" (v. 11).

*What about work?* So maybe work is the answer. Immerse yourself in your career. Set high goals, achieve all you can, make a name for yourself in your chosen profession. Solomon did that too. His wealth and wisdom earned him a worldwide reputation. But he soon discovered that work alone can't fill the void in a person's soul. When work is your god, your mind won't be at rest when you lie down to sleep at night; besides, eventually you'll retire or die and leave everything you've worked for to somebody else who didn't work for it. "This too is meaningless," said Solomon, probably with a sigh.

His conclusion? "I hated life" (vv. 17-26).

Have you ever felt that way? Is life simply a game of "trivial pursuit' in which we work and laugh and try to squeeze out a bit of joy before we grow old and die? And we're never quite satisfied with our current circumstances? The twelve-year-old wants to be sixteen, and the seventy-year-old wants to be thirty-five again. The worker longs to retire, but the retiree misses the respect he had at work. No matter our situation, we want something more. We want something *else.*

My friend Jim Bird asked questions like the ones Solomon asked.[16]

"Church was not a part of my life as a young man," Jim says. "I didn't know Jesus Christ as Savior or Lord. So I spent the better part of my life trying to fill the emptiness in me."

He married and fathered a son, but found that his relationships with his family didn't fill the void in his soul. A hard-driving entrepreneur in the real estate and construction business, Jim was a self-made millionaire by age twenty-six. His family bought fine houses, took European vacations, and drove big cars.

"Eventually I decided I was being selfish," Jim admits. "I needed to devote my time and energy to the people of my community." He did so much community service, eventually he received an award as one of the Outstanding Young Men in the Commonwealth of Kentucky (an honor he shared with corecipient United States Senator Mitch McConnell).

When Jim's friend the governor created a new Bureau of Public Properties, he asked Jim to head it up. "I had seven hundred employees, a near $1 billion budget, and I was twenty-nine years old," Jim recalls. But soon afterward, Jim entered a decade he says can only be described as desperate and futile."

"Nothing had filled that emptiness in me," he remembers. "I began buying personal things at a frantic pace. I was making repeated trips to Las Vegas and gambling tens of thousands of dollars. With partners I bought four banks. We built shopping centers, more than a thousand homes, a lumberyard, and a panel plant. We were racing thoroughbred horses all over the East coast. All in a desperate attempt to fill that emptiness."

Jim became addicted to alcohol and drugs. He was in the winner's circle for the 1985 Kentucky Derby and attended a party filled with dignitaries. "I know this because people told me," Jim says, "but I don't remember doing it. I experienced frequent blackouts."

He entered a treatment center and, with the Lord's help, hasn't taken a drink or another mind-altering drug since. He also began attending a support group called H.O.P.E. (He Offers Peace Everlasting), sponsored by Southland Christian Church in Lexington, Kentucky.

"I began the process of surrendering my life and my will to Jesus Christ," he explains. "I didn't consider myself worthy to enter the sanctuary of a church. But when we walked into Southland Christian Church, we were greeted with warm smiles, open arms, and loving hearts. They accepted us right where we were, and I'll be eternally grateful." Jim and his wife had finally found the one thing that could fill the void.

"I'm not going to suggest that my life was easy," he points out. "One word to describe when we first accepted Christ is *tumultuous*." Tumultuous but also victorious, as Jim and his wife continued to grow in the Lord with the help of mature Christians who shepherded and taught them.

Ultimately, Jim dismantled his business. Today he says, "The money's gone, but I'm rich in the things that matter! I'm a child of the King!"

Jim's minister at the time, Wayne Smith, befriended and discipled him. Eventually Jim went to Bible college—he was a straight-A student in classes I taught—and became a preacher himself. Today Jim Bird serves as senior minister of Fort Caroline Christian Church in Jacksonville, Florida. His life is a testimony to the saving, transforming power of God.

He says, "The church is not just a hospital for sinners; it is a MASH unit on the front lines, where the bruised and bleeding can be attended to by the Great Physician. Christians should consider ourselves 'Physician's Assistants.'"

Like Jim, the cynical King Solomon eventually grasped what life is all about. Reflecting on what he'd learned from his long quest, he advised young people: "Be happy . . . while you are young, and let your heart give you joy in the days of your youth. . . . But know that for all these things God will bring you to judgment. . . . Remember your Creator in the days of your youth, before the days of trouble come. . . . Fear God and keep his commandments, for this is the whole duty of man" (Ecclesiastes 11:9; 12:1, 13).

Life's most worthwhile goal is the quest to love the Lord our God with all our heart, soul, mind, and strength. Only the resurrected Lord Jesus can fill us with "living hope" (1 Peter 1:3). Only he can give us life "to the full" (John 10:10).

## I. Jesus—Who is he really?

On the day after Jesus fed more than five thousand people, many of his disciples grumbled when Jesus said, "I am the bread of life"—the spiritual nutrition a person needs to live forever. This was a hard teaching to understand and accept, so "many of his disciples turned back and no longer followed him" (John 6:48, 66).

But Jesus had been spending extra time teaching twelve of his disciples. Turning to them, Jesus asked a poignant question: "You do not want to leave too, do you?"

Simon Peter spoke for the rest of the group: "Lord, to whom shall we go? You have the words of eternal life. We believe and know that you are the Holy One of God" (vv. 67-69).

Peter was right. In the final analysis, the question isn't, "Where shall we go?" The question is, "To whom?"

The ultimate question in regard to the existence of God is simply, "Who is Jesus Christ?" If Jesus is who he claimed to be, then we not only know that God *exists*; we also know what God is *like*. "Anyone who has seen me has seen the Father," Jesus insisted (John 14:9). Jesus focused attention on this issue when he asked his disciples, "Who do you say I am?" (Matthew 16:15).

There are a number of evidences that thoughtful believers have offered in support of the existence of God. But my favorite is what I call the Jesus Argument, because Jesus personally embodies all that's best in each of the classic arguments:

**The Moral Argument** says there must be a God, for he is the source of a universal moral law—an inborn sense of what ought to be—that we find within ourselves.[17] *Jesus Christ is morality personified.* Not only did his teachings capture both the letter and the spirit of the moral law; he also lived it, embodied it, and perfectly fulfilled it.

**The Cosmological Argument** points to the principle of cause and effect and argues that God is the first cause (or uncaused cause), the source of all created things.[18] *Jesus Christ is the first cause personified.* "Without him nothing was made that has been made" (John 1:3). "By him all things were created" (Colossians 1:16).

**The Teleological Argument** points to the evidences of design and order in the universe and insists that God is the divine architect, or designer, who made all things to fulfill the purpose of his perfect will.[19] *Jesus Christ is purpose and order personified.* He "works out everything in conformity with the purpose of his will" (Ephesians 1:11).

**The Intuitional Argument** says there's something inside the heart of every human being that instinctively longs for God. *Jesus Christ came in person to fill the void.* "In him was life, and that life was the light of men" (John 1:4).

So who is Jesus really? What do *you* think? Jesus came to earth as a man, but he also insisted that he should be honored the same way we honor God the Father (John 5:23). His listeners recognized by things he did and said (such as "I and the Father are one") that he claimed to be "equal with God" (John 10:30-38; 5:17, 18). Further, Jesus claimed for himself—and was credited with having—attributes, powers, and honors that belong only to God:

- moral perfection (John 8:29, 46; 2 Corinthians 5:21; 1 Peter 2:22)
- eternal existence (John 8:58; 17:5; Hebrews 1:8; Revelation 1:4, 8, 17; 22:13)
- power to forgive sin (Mark 2:1-12)

- power to bestow life (John 11:25, 43, 44)
- authority to judge (Matthew 25:31-46; John 5:26, 27)

It's wrong, of course, to worship Satan (Matthew 4:10). It's wrong to worship human beings; even a great man like Peter refused to let Cornelius fall at his feet (Acts 10:25, 26). It's wrong to worship angels (Revelation 19:9, 10; 22:8, 9). But it's right to worship Jesus, the Lamb of God (Revelation 5:12). Thus, he's not a mere man or an angel; he is God. Jesus rightly accepted worship when his followers praised him (Matthew 9:18; 14:33; 28:9; John 9:35-38).

## J. Jesus—Why does the Bible call Jesus the only Son of God? Aren't we all God's children?

I've been asked the question this way:

*Jesus is said to be the only Son of God. But I've also been told that we are all children of God. Since the term* children *incorporates sons, then it follows that Jesus isn't the only one. Is this just a semantic argument, or is there really an inconsistency here?*

My response:

It's not just semantics, but there's no inconsistency. In one sense, we're all children of God by virtue of creation. Paul told the Athenians, "We are God's offspring" (Acts 17:29). But sin disrupted the relationship God desires to have with us, so we need to be "born again" or, to use a different analogy, "adopted" back into God's spiritual family (John 3:1-5; Romans 8:15-17; Galatians 4:1-7). There's a special sense in which we become God's children when we accept Christ as our Savior and are baptized into him. This is something we must decide for ourselves, not something others can decide for us (John 1:12, 13; Galatians 3:26-28).

Jesus is God's "one and only" Son. Since he is divine, he bears a unique relationship to the Father that you and I don't possess (John 1:14; 3:16).

But since he also came to earth as a real human being, he understands our humanity; and he's even willing to call us "brothers" (Hebrews 2:9-18).

## K. Jesus—What happened during the "missing years" of Jesus' life not recorded in the Bible?

That's another question you may be asked from time to time. Here's a response:

By "missing years" I presume you're talking about the years before Jesus' public ministry, which the Bible says he began when he was thirty years old (Luke 3:23). Actually, the Bible does tell us several facts about his early years, and many of the details are recorded in the Gospel of Luke, a book widely respected for its historical accuracy.

We know Jesus was born in Bethlehem and was "consecrated to the Lord" in Jerusalem as a baby in accordance with Old Testament law (Luke 2:1-38; see also Exodus 13:2, 12). After traveling to Egypt for a while to escape King Herod's violence, Joseph and Mary brought Jesus back to their hometown of Nazareth, a village in Galilee (Matthew 2:13-23). There Jesus grew up, we assume, much like other Jewish boys in his day. Luke simply records, "And the child grew and became strong; he was filled with wisdom, and the grace of God was upon him" (Luke 2:40). At age twelve he traveled with his parents to Jerusalem for the Passover Feast, and later "they found him in the temple courts, sitting among the teachers, listening to them and asking them questions." The Bible adds, "Everyone who heard him was amazed at his understanding and his answers."

When Mary questioned him, his response says a lot: "Didn't you know I had to be in my Father's house?" (Luke 2:46-49). He was only twelve, but he already knew where he belonged, who his real Father was, and what his priorities were.

It might seem strange that the Bible bypasses the next eighteen years and picks up the story of Jesus' life when he was baptized at age thirty. But there's another key verse that summarizes Jesus' years in between.

Luke 2:52 says, "Jesus grew in wisdom and stature, and in favor with God and men." Those years might appear to be "missing" from our perspective, but there was nothing missing from Jesus! He was the perfectly balanced individual, complete in every aspect of his life.

*He grew in wisdom.* During his ministry, Jesus frequently quoted Scripture and applied it in a fresh, memorable way that amazed his first-century listeners and still impresses us two thousand years later. How did he spend his "missing years"? It appears he spent some of the time studying, thinking, observing, and learning life lessons from his godly parents, Joseph and Mary (see v. 51).

*He grew in stature.* His physical body developed as ours do—from the soft skin and tiny limbs of vulnerable childhood to the muscular physique of a full-grown man. Jesus wasn't a wimp. Having grown up in a carpenter's home, it's reasonable to assume he was physically strong.

*He grew in favor (literally, in grace) with God.* He prayed a lot during his ministry (see Mark 1:35 and Luke 5:16, for example), so it's reasonable to conclude that he developed this habit during his youth. No doubt he also spent time pondering his mission and the way God's grace related to real people with real problems.

*He grew in favor with men.* Jesus wasn't a hermit. During his ministry he attended dinner parties, preached to throngs of thousands, and met one-on-one with powerful individuals like Nicodemus. How did he spend the years leading up to his ministry? Evidently by rubbing shoulders with friends and neighbors, interacting with others in social settings.

Non-canonical books (those not included in the Christian Scriptures) devote chapter after chapter to fanciful stories about Jesus' "childhood miracles" in a futile attempt to "fill in the gaps" of silence in the genuine Scriptures. But to me, the restraint exercised by the biblical authors is a testimony to the Bible's truthfulness and inspiration. Bonaventure had this to say about the relative quietness of Jesus' first thirty years: "His doing nothing wonderful was itself a kind of wonder. As there was power in His actions, so is there power in His silence."[20]

Jesus did too many things for anyone to write them all down. The Bible itself acknowledges, "Jesus did many other things as well" (John 21:25). But what is written is sufficient to convince us that Jesus is the Christ, the Son of God; and by believing, we can have life in his name (vv. 30, 31).

## L. Jesus' Resurrection—Why do Christians believe Jesus literally rose from the dead?[21]

During my years as a college professor, I began a class session with a true-false history quiz:

1. Millard Fillmore served as president of the United States. (true)
2. In 1945, the United States dropped atomic bombs on the Japanese cities of Hiroshima and Nagasaki. (true)
3. Sir Isaac Newton discovered the theory of relativity. (false)
4. The Declaration of Independence was signed by American patriots in 1776. (true)
5. A man in his early thirties was badly beaten and cut and pronounced legally dead. Three days later he was alive again.

The students paused at that final question, unsure how to answer it. Then I explained that the answer was unequivocally true, because I was referring to the resurrection of Jesus Christ.

If I had said "Christ rose from the dead," my Christian students would have been quick to say true, because we are accustomed to hearing the resurrection presented as a religious dogma. Actually it's a fact of history, just as real as World War II or the signing of the Declaration of Independence—supported by solid evidence and eyewitness testimony.

There's a lot at stake when we affirm the resurrection. If Jesus didn't rise from the dead, then he was a great teacher but nothing more. A dead Savior can't save anybody. But we need to take it even further. If the resurrection didn't happen, Jesus wasn't a great teacher at all, because he spoke often about the resurrection and pointed to it as the ultimate proof of his identity as the Messiah. If he didn't rise from the dead, then the Master Teacher was mistaken about his main message.

If Jesus didn't rise from the dead, the New Testament can't be trusted. The four Gospels would never have been written, for there would be no good news if the story of Jesus ended at the cross. There would be no book of Acts if there were no actual resurrection of Christ. The rest of the New Testament, from Romans to Revelation, was written to instruct and encourage believers to serve the risen Christ even in the face of persecution.

If Jesus didn't rise from the dead, the great ordinances of the Christian faith would be stripped of their meaning. Baptism would be nothing but an empty ceremony. The Lord's Supper would be a memorial to someone who is dead and gone, but not communion with someone who is very much alive. If Jesus didn't rise from the dead, we are fools for believing and perpetuating a lie. We are wasting our time when we sing his praises and invoke his name in prayer. "If Christ has not been raised, your faith is futile; you are still in your sins" (1 Corinthians 15:17).

But what does the evidence show?

Jesus' death on the cross is a fact of history, certified by an experienced Roman centurion familiar with killing (Mark 15:44, 45). Jesus' body was sealed inside a tomb in a public location under the watchful eyes of guards posted by the governor, but three days later the tomb was empty (Matthew 27:62–28:10). (The soldiers' duty was to guard a dead body, and they let him get away!) Over the next forty days, Jesus showed himself alive to a number of eyewitnesses and gave them "many convincing proofs that he was alive" (Acts 1:3). The reports of Jesus' post-resurrection appearances are numerous and credible.

In spite of their initial fears and doubts, Jesus' disciples couldn't deny his resurrection.

- He walked with them, talked with them, and ate broiled fish with them (Luke 24:36-43).
- Hundreds of witnesses saw the Lord alive; these were not fleeting glimpses, but prolonged interviews (1 Corinthians 15:3-6).
- Doubters like Thomas and skeptics like Saul of Tarsus and Jesus' half brother James turned to faith because of the resurrection (John 20:24-29; 1 Corinthians 15:7, 8). The phenomenal growth of the early church bears witness to the truth of the early Christians' message: "He is alive!" And in a Jewish culture where the Sabbath Day was highly regarded, only something as significant as the resurrection could cause the followers of Christ to begin gathering on the first day of the week to commune with their Lord.

So if the resurrection really happened, what then?

The resurrection of Jesus Christ towers above all other events in human history. It validates Jesus' claims about himself. He was "declared with power to be the Son of God by his resurrection from the dead" (Romans 1:4)—unique among all the religious leaders of the world. Because he conquered death for himself, he can conquer death for us. Our merciful God "has given us new birth into a living hope through the resurrection of Jesus Christ from the dead" (1 Peter 1:3).

## M. Miracles—Is it reasonable to believe the miracles described in the Bible actually happened?

Walking on water, healing the blind, raising the dead . . . Is it rea sonable to believe those things? Yes—if you allow for the possibility that on rare occasions the God who created nature intervenes and overrides a natural process by the exercise of divine will. Miracle don't violate the principle of cause and effect; they simply introduc a supernatural cause into the pattern. If God exists, miracles are at least a possibility.

To tell us about the nature and purpose of miracles, the New Testament writers used the following Greek words:

- *Dunameis* (from which we derive our word *dynamite*) means "mighty works." It emphasizes the power of God expressed in the miraculous act.
- *Terata* ("wonders") emphasizes the effect of the miracles. Those who observed these mighty deeds were filled with wonder and awe.
- *Semeia* (frequently used in the Gospel of John) is usually translated "signs," for it highlights the significance, meaning, or purpose of the miracles.[22]

Notice how these terms appear together in Scripture:

- "Jesus of Nazareth was a man accredited by God to you by miracles, wonders and signs" (Acts 2:22).
- "The things that mark an apostle—signs, wonders and miracles—were done among you with great perseverance" (2 Corinthians 12:12).
- "This salvation, which was first announced by the Lord, was confirmed to us by those who heard him. God also testified to it by signs, wonders and various miracles, and gifts of the Holy Spirit distributed according to his will" (Hebrews 2:3, 4).

Biblical miracles were not random magic tricks; they offered purposeful, credible evidence that God's message was trustworthy. For example, Nicodemus told Jesus, "Rabbi, we know you are a teacher who has come from God. For no one could perform the miraculous signs you are doing if God were not with him" (John 3:2).

By contending that miracles described in the Bible actually happened, we don't mean the world is a chaotic place where scientific laws are constantly disrupted. A miracle is a rare exception, not the rule. Jesus multiplied loaves of bread, but once eaten, the bread was digested in the normal way. Lazarus was raised from the dead, but then his body was once again subject to normal processes and pains. In fact (poor Lazarus), after he was resurrected, Jesus' enemies wanted to kill him again (John 12:9-11).

Some skeptics suppose the miracles recorded in the Bible were simply the invention of naive, unscientific minds; but ancient people weren't fools. When his virgin fiancée became pregnant, Joseph didn't need a degree in gynecology to know that babies don't come from the stork. James and John didn't understand twenty-first century meteorology, but they had sailed the Sea of Galilee long enough to recognize a miracle when Jesus instantly calmed a violent storm.

Others speculate that biblical miracles were psychologically induced; people weren't physically healed—they just felt better after encountering Jesus. However, it's impossible to explain biblical miracles as "mind over matter" or emotional manipulation, since they include things like giving sight to a man born blind, simultaneously healing ten men of leprosy, or raising the dead.

Plus, many miracles were performed publicly before large crowds (see Mark 1:33, 34, for example)—and even in the presence of skeptics who were not predisposed to believe, but who couldn't dispute the reality of the miracles (see Mark 3:1-6 and Acts 4:13-22, for example).

The Bible authors calmly and matter-of-factly reported the miracles performed by the Lord and his prophets and apostles.

Can we prove to a skeptic that those miracles really happened? Probably not. John tells us about some of the first-century observers: "Even after Jesus had done all these miraculous signs in their presence, they still would not believe in him" (12:37).

But if we read the Bible with an open mind and allow for the possibility of divine intervention, then we can recognize God's purpose and power in the signs and wonders recorded there. "Jesus did many other miraculous signs in the presence of his disciples, which are not recorded in this book. But these are written that you may believe that Jesus is the Christ, the Son of God, and that by believing you may have life in his name" (John 20:30, 31).

## N. Reincarnation—Why don't Christians believe in it?

A surprising number of Americans (between 20 and 24 percent, according to recent polls) have embraced reincarnation, the idea that we go through many cycles or lifetimes of birth, death, and rebirth.[22]

We read Pat's view in chapter 3: "I have no proof, but it makes a lot of sense. Why base judgment of a person for all eternity on one lifetime, when they might have been plunked down in rotten circumstances and died young? If I were designing a universe, I'd rotate beings through all sorts of different circumstances so that they would learn more."

Belief in reincarnation is rooted in Eastern religions (especially Hinduism). Space will not permit a thorough discussion of this question, but here are some observations and questions that I offered in my response to Pat:

*Reincarnation is intellectually unconvincing.* It lacks the kind of historical evidence that supports the resurrection of Christ, whose risen body was witnessed by hundreds of people (1 Corinthians 15:3-8).

*Reincarnation is emotionally unsatisfying.* Doesn't it lead to despair to think you're stuck in an ongoing cycle of lifetimes? How can you offer comfort to a person who's suffering if he's simply paying the price for sin in a past life? And if you aren't sure what form you will take in a future life, how can you have any real hope?

*Reincarnation is spiritually demoralizing.* Doesn't it make you feel depersonalized to think that there is no personal God who cares about you, that you're simply at the mercy of impersonal fate? Christ offers a personal relationship with a real heavenly Father, not a philosophy that tells you to lose your identity and become one with the universe.

*Reincarnation is morally uninspiring.* How can reincarnation motivate you to be a better person? After all, there's no proof a "good" person will come back in a better form—and ultimately, who can say what's "good" or "better" anyway, apart from the God described in the Bible?

*Reincarnation is socially unworkable.* The poor, the sick, the homeless . . . aren't they simply working out the consequences of bad karma? Why help them avoid the results of their own misdeeds? Have cultures dominated by belief in reincarnation developed superior ways of life?

*Reincarnation is unbiblical.* "Man is destined to die once, and after that to face judgment" (Hebrews 9:27).

## O. Salvation—Do we really need a Savior? Shouldn't we just accept responsibility for our own actions?

Don't be surprised to find that your friends are thinking seriously about questions like these. Here is a well-thought-out, frank presentation of how the salvation question has been posed to me:

*The "saving" aspect of Jesus never made sense to me. I've always believed he existed and that he was a great teacher and a very good example, but I still can't swallow the saving, for the following reasons:*

*1. It feels dishonorable to me. I don't think it's right when someone takes the rap for someone else—and the person he took the rap for usually doesn't learn anything from it.*

*2. It also feels a little like blackmail or bribery—like saying, "If you're nice to me, you don't get punished."*

*3. It seems to remove accountability from individuals for their actions. According to my sister (now a Christian), the only thing that gets you into Heaven is Jesus. I'd like to run the following scenario by you:*

> • *Person A is a scumbag who has been mean all his life. Then he repents, "gets Jesus" near the end, and gets into Heaven.*

- *Person B has been truly good all his life, tried to be nice, generous, and so forth. He doesn't "get Jesus," and doesn't get in.*

*I have trouble believing that person A finds greater favor in the eyes of God than person B. This also means that there is little incentive to behave oneself during the majority of one's life, since you obtain a "get out of jail free" card at a later date. In the words of Homer Simpson, "I'll repent on my deathbed."*

Here's how I began to answer those ideas regarding salvation:

You raise a number of important issues here. I agree with you on some points about Jesus:

- He did indeed live on earth, as extensive historical evidence demonstrates.
- He was indeed a great teacher, whose teachings amazed people then and still do now.
- He did indeed set a very good example.

However, Jesus must have been more than merely a good teacher and a good example, because the main focuses of his teaching concerned his own identity as the Son of God and his saving work on the cross. He didn't just say, "I've come to teach you a better way to live. Follow my example." He said, "I am the way and the truth and the life. No one comes to the Father except through me" (John 14:6). He summarized his life's purpose by saying, "The Son of Man did not come to be served, but to serve, and to give his life as a ransom for many" (Mark 10:45) and "The Son of Man came to seek and to save what was lost" (Luke 19:10).

He wasn't a good moral teacher if he was wrong about the central facts of his message. Josh McDowell has boiled it down to a three-*L* idea: Jesus is either a *liar* who knowingly misled people, a *lunatic* who meant well but misled people nonetheless, or the *Lord* who was indeed who he claimed to be.[23]

To me, the most reasonable alternative is to conclude that he's really the Lord.

Now, about the "saving" aspect of Christ's work. It seems to me that you've underestimated the seriousness of our sin problem. Even the "person who has been truly good all his life" still doesn't deserve to go to Heaven. One of theology professor Jack Cottrell's book titles states it well: *Being Good Enough Isn't Good Enough.* We're all in bigger trouble than you seem to assume, for even the best of us has fouled up big time. Comparing one person's righteous acts to another's is like saying, "Let's all jump into the Pacific Ocean and see who can swim to Hawaii first." Some of us might make it several miles, others only a few hundred yards, and I would sink like a rock! But none of us would make it to Hawaii by swimming. We need a boat or a plane to take us there. Likewise, we need a perfect Savior to take us to Heaven; we can't get there by our own strength, no matter how "good" we appear to be.

It also seems to me you've missed the whole idea of God's grace, which is at the core of the Christian gospel. If we got what we truly deserve, we'd all end up in Hell, for we've all done wrong and fallen short of God's perfect standards (Romans 3:23). In a sense, it *isn't* fair for someone else to "take the rap" for others who have done wrong. It's *more than* fair; it's grace.

Why should Jesus, who never sinned, endure unspeakable suffering on the cross because of our offenses? That's the marvel of God's love and mercy. This introduces a new and powerful incentive to, as you put it, "behave oneself during the majority of one's life." Instead of doing the right thing in a fearful, futile, guilt-ridden effort to please a demanding lawgiver, we're free to serve out of love and gratitude because he's forgiven and accepted us.

And by the way, Homer Simpson is treading on dangerous ground. Not everybody gets a chance to repent on his deathbed. It's hazardous to put off accepting Christ, since none of us knows exactly when we'll die. And there's no reason to wait. "Now is the time of God's favor, now is the day of salvation" (2 Corinthians 6:2).

I believe I offered some good answers there, but my questioner wasn't finished:

*But . . . God creates me imperfect, lands me in a lifetime guaranteed to test the imperfections of even the strongest person—then can't stand to look at me because I'm imperfect. Then tells me that he won't have anything to do with me unless I love his Son. This same Son he killed so that I don't have to pay the price for my actions—those same actions that I did because I am imperfect (and was created that way!). He also never gave me the choice of whether I wanted to do the time myself or have Jesus killed for me instead. If I could have picked, I would have spared Jesus. What happens to us "unsaved" who feel they should pay the price for their own actions themselves?*

My response:

Wait a minute. God didn't "create you imperfect." The Bible says, "Everything God created is good" (1 Timothy 4:4; see also Genesis 1:31). Though God doesn't let us decide whether to be born into this world, we're born with free will to choose right or wrong. "When tempted, no one should say, 'God is tempting me.' For God cannot be tempted by evil, nor does he tempt anyone; but each one is tempted when, by his own evil desire, he is dragged away and enticed" (James 1:13, 14).

The world is messed up because humans make foolish choices. We can't fix things without God's help. Occasionally we hear about a coal-mining tragedy in which miners end up trapped in a collapsed mine. They dug the hole themselves; once the roof caves in, they can't dig their way out. They won't be saved without a rescue effort from outside. Likewise, we've dug ourselves into our own problems, and when life caves in around us, we need a Savior from outside to dig us out. That's exactly what Jesus came to do.

No, God didn't let us decide whether or not he should send Jesus to save us. He took the initiative, out of love, instead of requiring us to "pay the price" for our own actions. But God didn't "have Jesus killed" in the way you've perceived it. God himself, *through Christ,* came to personally intervene. "[God] appeared in a body" (1 Timothy 3:16). "The Word [*that's Jesus*] was God. . . . The Word became flesh" (John 1:1, 14).

We are given the freedom to decide whether we will accept Christ. He doesn't force himself on us. To use a couple of biblical analogies, he stands at the door and knocks (Revelation 3:20), waiting for us to open the door. He offers us "living water" (John 4:10), but he won't force us to drink.

If Hell is real (as the Bible says), none of us would logically choose to "do the time ourselves"! That's the genius of God's grace and love. Christ "bore our sins in his body" when he died on the cross (1 Peter 2:24). He took the pain he didn't deserve (death) so we could receive a gift we don't deserve (eternal life).

# Notes

## Getting Started

1. Eddie Cantor, www.quotationsbook.com.

## Chapter 1

Epigraph. Ronald Reagan, www.brainyquote.com.

1. H. G. Wells, http://www.dabar.org/Homiletics/Expository/Eph5.htm.
2. Immanuel Kant, *Critique of Pure Reason* (New York: Willey Book Co., 1900). Quote found at http://www.fullbooks.com.
3. http://www.crandallu.ca/courses/grphil/Introd.htm.
4. Joseph Joubert, www.searchquotes.com.

## Chapter 2

Epigraph. George Carlin, www.brainyquote.com.

1. For more of these, read "20 Everyday Expressions That Come from the Bible" in *Discovering God's Story* by Jim Eichenberger (Cincinnati, OH: Standard Publishing, 2010), 219–221.
2. Lincoln and Newton quotes, http://www.why-the-bible.com/bible.htm.
3. Aldous Huxley, http://www.sciencedoubts.com.
4. Norman Geisler and Ronald Brooks, *When Skeptics Ask* (Wheaton, IL: Victor Books, 1990 edition), 201.
5. Strabo, *Geography*. Book XVII, section 54, http://penelope.uchicago.edu/Thayer/E/Roman/Texts/Strabo/17A3*.html.
6. Edward Meyer, professor, University of Berlin, considered one of the greatest living authorities on anciet history, http://www.why-the-bible.com/bible.htm.
7. Josephus, *The Works of Josephus* (complete and unabridged), translated by William Whiston (Peabody, MA: Hendrickson Publishers, new updated edition 1987), 523.
8. http://www.textexcavation.com/suetoniustestimonium.html.
9. There is some debate about whether Drusilla was a granddaughter or, rather, a great-granddaughter of Antony and Cleopatra. See http://www.tyndalehouse.com/egypt/ptolemies/selene_ii.htm.

10. http://www.answers.com/topic/cyrus-ii-of-persia.

11. For further explanation of Nahum's prophecy about Nineveh, see James Montgomery Boice, *The Minor Prophets: An Expositional Commentary*, Vol. 2 (Grand Rapids, MI: Zondervan, 1986), 57–72.

12. For a detailed explanation of Ezekiel's prophecy about Tyre, see James Smith, *Ezekiel*, Bible Study Textbook Series (Joplin, MO: College Press, 1984), 307–317.

13. http://focusonjerusalem.com/thefallofjerusalem.html.

14. Information in this section was taken from Peter Spielmann, "Grove of Prehistoric Pines a Startling Australian Find," *Cincinnati Enquirer*, December 15, 1994.

15. http://www.latinvulgate.com.

16. Johannes Kepler, http://www.icr.org/article/scientific-progress.

17. Mark Twain, http://www.tentmaker.org.

# Chapter 3

1. Conversations with Pat (not her real name) are taken from author correspondence. Used with permission.

2. Theodor Christlieb, *Modern Doubt and Christian Belief* (New York: Charles Scribner's Sons, 1874), 143–144, http://books.google.com.

3. J. B. Phillips, *Your God Is Too Small* (New York: Macmillan Publishing Co., Inc., 1973), table of contents, http://books.google.com.

4. For a helpful in-depth discussion of the attributes of God, see *What the Bible Says About God the Creator* by Jack Cottrell (Eugene, OR: Wipf & Stock Publishers, 2001).

5. Michael Gerson, "A Search That Goes Beyond Physics," *Cincinnati Enquirer*, December 26, 2011.

6. Haldane and Knox, http://www.todayinsci.com/QuotationsCategories/H_Cat/Haldane_John-Quotations.htm.

7. Francis Schaeffer, http://www.rationalpi.com/theshelter/live.html.

8. Blaise Pascal, www.brainyquote.com.

9. For an interesting look at the historical evidence for the claims of Christ, see *The Case for Christ* by Lee Strobel (Grand Rapids, MI: Zondervan, 1998). A still-useful older book that introduces people to Christ is *More Than a Carpenter* by Josh McDowell (Grand Rapids, MI: Tyndale House Publishers, Inc., 1977, 2004).

10. C. S. Lewis, *Mere Christianity* copyright © C. S. Lewis Pte. Ltd. 1942, 1943, 1944, 1952. (New York: Simon & Schuster / first Touchstone edition 1996), 56. Extract reprinted by permission.

11. Information in this section was taken from the author's personal communication and is used with permission. Names have been changed.

# Chapter 4

Epigraph. Martin Luther King Jr., www.thinkexist.com.

1. Information in this section is taken from author correspondence. Used with permission.

2. Johann Wolfgang von Goethe, www.ranker.com.

3. Os Guinness, *In Two Minds: The Dilemma of Doubt and How to Resolve It* (Downers Grove, IL: InterVarsity Press, 1976), 63–64. See also Bertrand Russell, *Why I Am Not a Christian* (New York: Simon & Schuster, 1957).

4. Os Guinness, *God in the Dark: The Assurance of Faith Beyond a Shadow of a Doubt* (Wheaton, IL: Crossway Books, 1996), 23.

5. Rene Descartes, www.wisdomquotes.com.

6. C. S. Lewis, *Mere Christianity* copyright © C. S. Lewis Pte. Ltd. 1942, 1943, 1944, 1952. (New York: Simon & Schuster / first Touchstone edition 1996), 124–125. Extract reprinted by permission.

7. Blaise Pascal, www.tentmaker.org.

8. Guinness, *God in the Dark,* 148.

9. http://www.preceptaustin.org/hebrews_46-7.htm.

10. Guinness, *In Two Minds,* 224–225.

11. F. F. Bosworth, www.tentmaker.org.

12. For an insightful analysis of the strengths and weaknesses of Pascal's Wager, see http://www.peterkreeft.com/topics/pascals-wager.htm.

13. Information in this section is taken from author correspondence with Paul and David. Used with permission.

14. Charlotte Elliott, http://www.hymnsite.com/lyrics/umh357.sht.

# Chapter 5

Epigraph. Winston Churchill, www.thinkexist.com.

1. Information in this section and at the end of the chapter is taken from author correspondence with Audrey Stout. Used with permission.

2. The story of Sue Ann (not her real name) is taken from author correspondence. Used with permission.

3. The name and details in this story have been changed.

4. William Shakespeare, *Romeo and Juliet* (Act 2, Scene II), http://www.online-literature.com/shakespeare/romeo_and_juliet/10.

5. www.m-w.com.

6. I deal more fully with the problem of suffering in my book *Faith Under Fire: Studies from First & Second Peter* (Joplin, MO: College Press, 2002), 105–121.

7. Glandion Carney and William Long, *Trusting God Again: Regaining Hope After Disappointment or Loss* (Downers Grove, IL: InterVarsity Press, 1995), 95.

8. C. S. Lewis, *The Problem of Pain* (New York: Macmillan, 16th printing 1975), 93. Extract reprinted by permission.

9. R. T. Kendall, *The Thorn in the Flesh* (Lake Mary, FL: Charisma House / Strang, 2004), 8.

10. Tom Lawson, "How Could God Let This Happen?" *The Lookout,* December 8, 1996. Reused with permission.

11. Bob Russell, "When Life Isn't Fair," *Christian Standard,* June 14, 1981. Reused with permission.

## Chapter 6

Epigraph. Artemus Ward, www.thinkexist.com.

1. Information in this section is taken from author conversations with Yoshi and Emiko. Used with permission.

2. W. Somerset Maugham, www.thinkexist.com.

3. William Barclay, *The Gospel of Mark* (Philadelphia: The Westminster Press, revised edition 1975), 165.

4. Josh McDowell and Don Stewart, *Answers to Tough Questions,* www.josh.org.

5. It could be argued that every ethnic group contributes something positive to our overall understanding of what it means for human beings to be created in the image of God. Perhaps that's why "the glory and honor of the nations" will be brought into Heaven (Revelation 21:26). At the same time, there may be unique temptations in every culture (materialism, intellectual pride, sensuality, self-sufficiency, or superstition) that make it vulnerable to the devil's wiles. Once institutionalized by decades or centuries of tradition, do these customs harden into strongholds of Satan's power?

6. Information in this section is based on the true story related to the author by Bob Russell, retired senior minister of Southeast Christian Church in Louisville, Kentucky, about his own personal interviews with Nabeel. More details appeared in "Former Muslim Now Embraces and Defends Christianity," *Southeast Outlook* (November 17, 2011), 20, 25. An even fuller account appears on Nabeel Qureshi's website, http://answering-islam.org/Authors/Qureshi/testimony.htm.

## Chapter 7

1. David Kinnaman and Gabe Lyons, *Unchristian: What a New Generation Really Thinks About Christianity . . . and Why It Matters* (Grand Rapids, MI: Baker Books, 2007), 42.

2. Ibid., 48.

3. "Umpire Is Charged in Theft of Cards," AP article, *Cincinnati Enquirer,* April 25, 1990.

4. "Churchgoer's Foul Language Burns Fellow Worker's Ears," Dear Abby column, *Cincinnati Enquirer,* March 29, 1990.

5. Sheldon Vanauken, *A Severe Mercy* (San Francisco: HarperSanFrancisco / Harper Collins, 1980), 85.

6. W. Carl Ketcherside, *The Royal Priesthood* (St. Louis, MO: Mission Messenger, 1956), 2.

7. www.m-w.com.

8. http://www.usnews.com/news/politics/articles/2008/01/17/remarks-of-the-ages.

9. Rubel Shelly, *Prepare to Answer: A Defense of the Christian Faith* (Grand Rapids, MI: Baker Books, 1990), 17.

10. R. C. Sproul provides a helpful explanation of this point in *Reason to Believe* (Grand Rapids, MI: Lamplighter Books / Zondervan, 1982), 76–81.

11. Ibid., 82–83.

12. G. K. Chesterton, www.brainyquote.com.

13. Robert Shannon. Used with permission.

14. Information in this section was provided by Darrell and Maria Thompson. Used with permission.

15. See www.joniandfriends.org.


## Chapter 8

Epigraph. Francis Schaeffer, www.brainyquote.com.

1. "Top Trends of 2011: Changing Role of Christianity," http://www.barna.org/faith-spirituality/543-top-trends-of-2011-changing-role-of-christianity.

2. Ravi Zacharias, "An Ancient Message, Through Modern Means, to a Postmodern Mind," *Just Thinking,* http://www.rzim.org/justthinkingfv/tabid/602/articleid/6589/cbmoduleid/881/default.aspx.

3. February 12, 2002, article at http://www.barna.org/barna-update/article/5-barna-update/67-americans-are-most-likely-to-base-truth-on-feelings.

4. Kinnaman and Lyons, *UnChristian,* 182.

5. Ibid., 83.

6. www.learnersdictionary.com.

7. John Lennon, www.brainyquote.com.

8. Information in this section is taken from author correspondence. Used with permission.

9. www.m-w.com.

10. http://www.schoolprayerinamerica.info/1separationchurchstate.html.

11. Charles Colson and Nancy Pearcey, *How Now Shall We Live?* (Wheaton, IL: Tyndale House, 1999), 23.

12. Paul Copan, *"True for You But Not for Me": Deflating the Slogans That Leave Christians Speechless* (Minneapolis, MN: Bethany House Publishers, 1998), 35. Copan is actually quoting Maurice Cranston, "Toleration" in *Encyclopedia of Philosophy,* volume 8, Paul Edwards, editor (New York: Free Press / Macmillan, 1967), 143. Cranston maintains that toleration "implies the existence of something believed to be disagreeable"; it "has an element of condemnation built into its meaning."

13. Ibid., 35.

14. Ibid., 37.

15. www.brainyquote.com.

16. These ideas about permissiveness, persecution, and persuasion are credited to former senator Dan Coats in "The Challenges College Students Face on Secular Campuses" by Steve Singleton, http://www.doesgodexist.org/MayJun98/TheChallengesCollege StudentsFaceOnSecularCampuses.html.

17. Timothy Keller, *The Reason for God: Belief in an Age of Skepticism* (New York: Dutton / Penguin, 2008), 12.

18. Information in this section is taken from author correspondence. Used with permission.

19. Will Rogers, www.thinkexist.com.

20. Information in this section is taken from author correspondence. Used with permission.


## Appendix One

1. Tertullian, http://www.ntcanon.org/Tertullian.shtml.

2. H. L. Mencken, www.brainyquote.com.

3. Clark H. Pinnock, *Set Forth Your Case: Studies in Christian Apologetics* (Chicago: Moody Press, eighth printing 1976), 11.

4. Oswald Chambers, *My Utmost for His Highest*, 125. Edited by James Reimann, © 1992 by Oswald Chambers Publications Assn., Ltd. Original edition © 1935 by Dodd Mead & Co., renewed 1963 by the Oswald Chambers Publications Assn., Ltd., and is used by permission of Discovery House Publishers, Box 3566, Grand Rapids, MI 49501. All rights reserved.

5. Pinnock, 73.

6. I was put onto the idea of dividing beliefs into categories by Rubel Shelly's book *Prepare to Answer: A Defense of the Christian Faith* (Grand Rapids, MI: Baker Book House, 1990), 18–20.

7. Jack Cottrell. Used with permission.

8. "The Crucifixion," *U.S. News & World Report,* April 16, 1990, 50.

9. Geisler and Brooks, *When Skeptics Ask,* 206.

10. Ravi Zacharias, *Can Man Live Without God?* (Dallas, TX: Word Publishing, 1994), 10–14.


## Appendix Two

1. *The NIV Exhaustive Concordance,* Edward W. Goodrick and John R. Kohlenberger III editors (Grand Rapids, MI: Zondervan Publishing House, 1990).

2. http://www.answers.com/topic/johannes-gutenberg.

3. http://www.unitedbiblesocieties.org.

4. http://apostlesofapollo.com/first-lunar-bible.

5. Information in this section is taken from author correspondence. Used with permission.

6. Freud argued that belief in God grows out of our childhood relationship with our parents. We must grant, of course, that there is some truth to this. Parents do shape a child's view of God during the child's early years, and Christian parents do their best to introduce their children to the true God. But according to Freud's view, faith in God springs from a childish wish for a heavenly protector to shield us from "the crushingly superior force of nature" (famines, earthquakes, hurricanes, and diseases); to assure that justice is done when other people violate our rights; and to help us cope with "the painful riddle of death, against which no medicine has yet been found, nor probably will be."

"When the growing individual finds that he is destined to remain a child for ever, that he can never do without protection against strange superior powers," Freud wrote, "he lends those powers the features belonging to the figure of his father; he creates for himself the gods whom he dreads, whom he seeks to propitiate, and whom he nevertheless entrusts with his own protection. Thus his longing for a father is a motive identical with his need for protection against the consequences of his human weakness."

Religious doctrines, Freud concluded, "are illusions and insusceptible of proof. No one can be compelled to think them true, to believe in them." See Sigmund Freud, *The Future of an Illusion,* edited by James Strachey (Garden City, NY: Anchor Books / Doubleday, revised Anchor Books edition 1964). Quotations checked at www.alfanos.org /pdfs/04_issues_philo_fall08/08_freud.pdf.

7. Karl Marx, http://conservapedia.com/Karl_Marx.

8. Bertrand Russell, *Why I Am Not a Christian* (New York: Simon & Schuster, 1957), 22.

9. See C. S. Lewis, *Mere Christianity* (New York: Simon & Schuster / first Touchstone edition 1996), 121.

10. Sproul, *Reason to Believe,* 73.

11. Ibid., 70.

12. Bertrand Russell, 17.

13. Information in this section is taken from author correspondence. Used with permission.

14. Wayne A. Meeks, *The First Urban Christians: The Social World of the Apostle Paul* (New Haven, CT: Yale University Press, second edition 1983), 181.

15. R. J. Kidwell, *Ecclesiastes* (in a single volume with Don DeWelt, *Song of Solomon*) (Joplin, MO: College Press, 1977), 9–10.

16. Jim Bird presented his full testimony at the North American Christian Convention in St. Louis, Missouri, on June 26, 1998. Information in this section is from that testimony. Audio tapes of Jim's message are available from Christian Audio Tapes (1-888-228-2737). His story is used with permission.

17. C. S. Lewis deals with this idea extensively in *Mere Christianity* (New York: Simon & Schuster / first Touchstone edition 1996), 17–39.

18. See Norman Geisler, *Christian Apologetics* (Grand Rapids, MI: Baker Book House, 1976), 237–259.

19. See Batsell Barrett Baxter, *I Believe Because . . .* (Grand Rapids, MI: Baker Book House, 1971), 59–73.

20. Bonaventure. Quoted in *Texts Explained* by Frederic William Farrar (New York: Dodd, Mead and Company, 1899), page 67 at www.books.google.com.

21. The material in this section is adapted from my "First Look" article in *The Lookout*, April 8, 2007.

22. *Smith's Bible Dictionary*, http://www.godrules.net/library/smith/NEWsmith13.htm.

23. See http://www.nytimes.com/2010/08/29/fashion/29PastLives.html and http://www.pewforum.org/Other-Beliefs-and-Practices/Many-Americans-Mix-Multiple-Faiths.aspx and http://www.cbsnews.com/stories/2011/05/15/sunday/main20063019.shtml.

24. Josh McDowell website, http://www.josh.org/site/apps/nlnet/content2.aspx?c=ddKDIMNtEqG&b=4340727&ct=5697377.

# About the Author

Read David's weekly column, "Revealed and Relevant," in *The Lookout* magazine, www.lookoutmag.com.

## Other Books by David Faust

*Monday Morning Prayers*
*Monday Morning Insights*
*Unquenchable Faith*
*Married for Good*
*Faith Under Fire*